Asleep in Heaven's Nursery

Asleep in Heaven's Nursery

TOMMY MANN

Tate Publishing & *Enterprises*

Asleep in Heaven's Nursery
Copyright © 2011 by Tommy Mann. All rights reserved.

No part of this publication may be reproduced, stored in a retrieval system or transmitted in any way by any means, electronic, mechanical, photocopy, recording or otherwise without the prior permission of the author except as provided by USA copyright law.

Scripture quotations are taken from the *Holy Bible, King James Version*, Cambridge, 1769. Used by permission. All rights reserved.

This book is designed to provide accurate and authoritative information with regard to the subject matter covered. This information is given with the understanding that neither the author nor Tate Publishing, LLC is engaged in rendering legal, professional advice. Since the details of your situation are fact dependent, you should additionally seek the services of a competent professional.

The opinions expressed by the author are not necessarily those of Tate Publishing, LLC.

Published by Tate Publishing & Enterprises, LLC
127 E. Trade Center Terrace | Mustang, Oklahoma 73064 USA
1.888.361.9473 | www.tatepublishing.com

Tate Publishing is committed to excellence in the publishing industry. The company reflects the philosophy established by the founders, based on Psalm 68:11,
"The Lord gave the word and great was the company of those who published it."

Book design copyright © 2011 by Tate Publishing, LLC. All rights reserved.
Cover design by Kenna Davis
Interior design by Christina Hicks

Published in the United States of America

ISBN: 978-1-61777-557-4
1. Religion / Christian Life / Death, Grief, Bereavement
2. Health & Fitness / Pregnancy & Childbirth
11.04.27

Dedication

This book is dedicated to our little miracle, Reagan. God completed our lives when He gave you to us. In loving memory of all our babies who are asleep in heaven's nursery.

www.tommymannministries.com

For this child I prayed, and the Lord has given me my petition which I asked of him.

1 Samuel 1:27

Acknowledgments

Dr. Warren and staff (especially Lindsay, Hope, and Pamela)—Piedmont Women's Clinic

Drs. Scardo, Vermillion, and Laye—Spartanburg Regional's Maternal/Fetal Medicine

Dr. Murdock and staff—Foothills Nephrology

Dr. Oloufa—Health Central, Orlando

Dr. Parra—Palmetto Pediatrics

The staff of Spartanburg Regional NICU and Greenville Memorial Pediatric

Everyone who shared a testimony

Table of Contents

Dedication	5
Acknowledgments	7
Our Story	11
It's Not Your Fault	27
When Does a Life Become a Life?	33
Is My Baby Really in Heaven?	43
What about My Aborted Baby?	65
Coping with Comments	75
My Advice	79
Testimonies	85
Appendix	103

Our Story

"Tommy…Tommy, wake up. It was blue. I'm pregnant." Although it usually takes me a few minutes to comprehend information that soon after waking up, I immediately became very excited. I didn't want to get too far ahead of myself, so I told Alicia to take another test just to be sure.

It was blue.

I had looked forward to being a father for several years, and there in the early morning of our Fort Worth apartment, my mind began to race ahead to many images: teaching my son how to shoot a basketball, walking my daughter down the aisle on her wedding day, and teaching my children to love God and the Florida Gators. It was finally starting to happen, and just to make it even more special, it was just two days until Mother's Day, which naturally made it even more special for my wife. Plus, neither of us would have to buy our mothers a gift now; we just had to give them the good news.

I was just weeks away from my college graduation and our big move to my home town of Orlando, Florida. As our trip drew closer, Alicia began to bleed a little, and we worried. We were able to take comfort in the stories people were telling us of how they bled early on and everything was fine. However, that little amount of bleeding continued on for over a week, so a nurse told us to come in for an appointment.

I'll never forget that time spent in the ultrasound room. What probably lasted only a few minutes felt like hours as I stood there in silence praying to see a heartbeat. Even though I didn't really know what a heartbeat would look like, the nurse's silence was not too reassuring. She turned the machine off, and when I asked for some results, she said she had to get the doctor.

The doctor came in and told us there was no heartbeat, and in that moment I almost lost my own. My knees felt as if they were ready to give out; I wanted to cry. I wanted to throw up. I wanted to go home. But most of all I wanted to make Alicia feel better, a task I soon realized I could never fully accomplish.

Because her hormone counts continued to increase, the doctors began to fear that Alicia's pregnancy may have been ectopic or tubal, both of which carried serious risks for the mother. The doctor wanted more blood work done and another ultrasound—two days before our move to Orlando.

The results of those tests were faxed to our new doctor in Florida. Between those results and tests from the new doctor, they came to the conclusion that Alicia had a septated uterus, which means there is a dividing wall that should not be there that almost divides her uterus in half. At any time during a pregnancy, the baby could attach himself to that septum and ultimately end his short life. That, they concluded, must have been what happened.

They scheduled a D&C so that everything could safely be removed, but one last ultrasound was ordered so that the doctor would know exactly where to look. During this ultrasound, the most amazing thing happened: we saw a heartbeat. And again, I almost lost mine. We went back to the doctor with the results, and she prescribed prenatal vitamins and another checkup.

We told everybody. We called every relative, every friend, telling them all about the miracle that occurred in the hospital. One person even jokingly told me, "You should write a book about that." Alicia started taking her vitamins and reading about what she should expect in the coming weeks. The doctor even gave us a due date, January 21, one day before my twenty-second birthday.

My dream of being a father was back on track. Life was good. I had just graduated from college, I had a great wife, I had several prospects for positions at churches, and now, through a miracle, a baby really was on the way.

That excitement only lasted a few more days. Alicia started bleeding again, but this time it wasn't just a little. Not wanting to take a chance, we immediately got in the car and made the thirty-minute drive to the emergency room. We sat there for hours before we were finally called back to a room.

There we were again in seemingly eternal silence as the nurse was probing in ultrasound. Just as I feared would happen, she turned off the machine and said she had to get the doctor. My head was spinning; I had the same feelings as before back in Texas. I wanted to cry, throw up, and just go home, but before I could say anything, Alicia looked at me with tears in her eyes and told me she needed me to be strong for her.

The doctor came in and confirmed what we already knew was true, and eventually we were released to go home. Alicia cried the whole way, but God granted my only request that night: to make me strong for her. When we got home, she went to bed, exhausted, and went right to sleep. As soon as I could tell she was asleep, the dam in my eyes broke, and I cried all night until my alarm went off for me to go to work the next morning.

The following week she had the D&C; there was no miracle heartbeat this time. The procedure at first was optional, but as Alicia's hemoglobin drastically dropped, the procedure became an emergency. We knew all the statistics about how the vast majority of women who have had miscarriages carry their second pregnancy to term, but those stats brought no comfort when the doctor came out to the waiting room and confirmed that our baby had in fact attached to the septum of Alicia's uterus. We now had to come to grips with what we were up against: a septum in a uterus that was already too small.

We had to let the healing process begin, which was difficult due to all the words of "encouragement" from well-meaning people.

"I guess it just wasn't the right time."

"We just want a healthy baby, and that one didn't seem like it would be healthy."

"At least it happened sooner rather than later."

And as all women do after these events, Alicia blamed herself. I would constantly ask her who created her body, including her uterus. She knew that God had and that he did not make a mistake, and this knowledge of the sovereignty of God was very beneficial for the recovery process.

A month later the doctor wanted to try a hysteroscopy, an operation very similar to a D&C that allowed the doctor to get a better look at the septum in the uterus. If it were thin enough, she would try to shave the septum away, but if it were too thick, she would have to leave it alone. To our dismay, the doctor came out with the news that the septum was a thick muscle that could not be removed. To top it off, the left side of her uterus was now thought to be too small to carry a developing baby. This news was hard to handle, but we continued to remind ourselves that God didn't make a mistake. Alicia's body was fearfully and wonderfully made, and God should be praised for it.

Six months passed. Alicia had healed physically, and we were healing emotionally. Two more blue tests brought the news that we were half hoping for. While we wanted another try, there was a very real, almost paralyzing fear of a repeat set of circumstances. We held out hope though because we knew that the second time is a charm for most women. Instead of a Mother's Day surprise, this late December announcement was going to be a Christmas surprise.

The only difference was this time we only told a few friends and family members. That made it easier to deal with when Alicia started bleeding again. This time there was no need to go to the doctor; we simply decided to let everything happen on its own. Now we were beginning to realize that our first loss was not just some fluke mishap but that an untreatable medical situation stood in our way of parenthood.

The third time it happened was quicker and much earlier on. It was a conception that implanted immediately on the septum of the uterus and never had a chance of survival. Although this one was easier to deal with from a physical standpoint, I hit rock bottom with my faith. This frustrated me because my faith in hard times was what had helped me out in so many situations up to this point. With this miscarriage, it seemed as if the Lord were trying to kick us while we were down; as the new pastor of students at a church in South Carolina, I was on a trip with Alicia to Chuck E. Cheese's with our three- through five-year-olds when the bleeding started.

Although I did not admit it to anyone until more than a year later, my dream of being a father was also lost there that day. I told myself that it was never going to happen, and from that day on, I stopped praying for a baby.

A Fourth Chance

Thank God for a praying woman! When the man of the house ceases to be the spiritual leader of the home, the wife has to step up. My wife stepped up her prayers for a baby where mine fell short. I didn't realize it, but she continued to beg God for the baby that we so badly wanted.

Two months later, Alicia came to me crying. She said she was pregnant but the process had already started; the bleeding had begun. We didn't realize it at the time, but the bleeding was caused by implantation, which, for the first time, was a good thing. Several weeks passed, and all along Alicia believed she was still carrying a baby, but she never told me as to not get my hopes up again. The time came for her first doctor appointment, which I thought was just for the doctor to confirm another miscarriage so we could be referred to a specialist. To my surprise, we went in for an ultrasound, and there we saw a tiny heartbeat, something we had only seen once back in Orlando.

Because of our history, the doctor decided that we should go for frequent visits. These appointments started out two weeks apart, but that didn't last long. From almost the beginning, we were driving forty-five minutes to the doctor every Friday.

Around the tenth week of the pregnancy, we were told to go to an appointment with the specialists at the maternal/fetal medicine office. It was at this first visit that the news was broken to us that Alicia had glomerulonephritis, which is a generic way of saying chronic renal failure. In layman's terms, her kidneys were only functioning at thirty-five percent.

So now we had a woman ten weeks pregnant who had an undersized, misshaped uterus; kidney disease; high blood pressure; and low hemoglobin levels. In addition to going to her doctor every Friday, we were now going to see the specialists every Tuesday, plus periodic visits to a nephrologist and a hematologist. The daily medication that Alicia had to take would have been considered a feast in many countries. In addition to the usual prenatal vitamin, she was also daily taking blood pressure medicine, a baby aspirin, and a folic acid supplement. Twice a day she was drinking a solution to neutralize potassium to help her kidneys, and she was taking two iron supplements. To top it off, she was taking twelve sodium bicarbonate pills a day.

Just finding food to eat became a chore. One doctor put Alicia on a sodium-restricted diet while another one put her on a low potassium diet. Because of her anemia, we had been trying to find foods that were high in iron, like beans, but beans are also high in potassium. It seemed that everything we tried to eat was either too high in sodium or potassium, so we had to be creative with our cooking.

One day after Alicia had gone in for some blood work, the doctor's office called her and said that she needed to get to the emergency room right away and have some more blood drawn. Her hemoglobin had dropped below 7.0, which was very dangerous. This led one of the specialists at the maternal/fetal medicine office to suggest a new treatment option: erythropoietin injections, or EPO for short. EPO is a hormone that is produced in the kidneys that helps the body store iron. Obviously Alicia's kidneys were not performing this task, which was why she was still so anemic despite taking high doses of iron supplements for the past several years.

The problem with the EPO injections is that, according to this doctor, there had never been a case in which a pregnant woman had received the treatment. He had to go over the risks of the treatment, the greatest of which was the unknown factor. Even though he strongly recommended it, he didn't exactly give us a lot of time to make a decision; he said if we agreed to it, he would set up the treatment the next morning.

For us, it was a no-brainer. We had already been praying that God would heal Alicia's anemia, and this new treatment seemed like a godsend to us. We showed up the next morning, and Alicia received the injection into the back of her arm, despite the fact that two nurses tried to talk her out of it. The injections went very well, and they became part of the regular routine of medication.

To the doctors, everything seemed so bad, but to us, every doctor appointment just got us one day closer to the due date. The doctors and their staffs began to cheer us on as we became regulars in their waiting rooms and offices. As one of the specialists put it, "We just don't see cases like this too often." And he wasn't joking. At the tenth week, one doctor suggested terminating the pregnancy, and later another doctor advised us that if we wanted children, then we needed to adopt them.

But as the due date drew closer, things began to look better; then came the day that one doctor decided to schedule her birth at the thirty-seventh week—just three weeks away. On the thirty-seventh week, we went to all of our appointments as usual, and without exception, every doctor admitted that they never thought we would make it to that point. The final point on the checklist was the amniocentesis, the test to see if the baby's lungs were mature enough to deliver. The test came back bearing good news, and we were admitted into the hospital that night for an induction the next morning.

We went in a night early so the doctors could give Alicia something to begin the process of softening her cervix so that the induction would go faster. She was induced into labor early the next morning, and before lunch, her water broke and the epidural was in. We were beating the odds and about to have a baby. But every time the nurses would check her cervix, they found only minimal progress. As evening came, the baby's heart rate began to drop with each contraction, but the doctor came by and told us he was not worried.

I tried not to let on that I was worried, but I felt so sick that I thought I was going to pass out. Fortunately the monitor was not in a place where Alicia could see it, which allowed me to make up numbers when she asked what the heart rate was. I believe lying to be a sin, but I told Alicia the baby's heart rate was 124 when it was really only 85. I have since repented.

At eight that night, the doctor who wasn't worried the hour before came back to check on us, and I'll never forget him saying, "I'm worried about your baby." The next fifty minutes were a blur, but I remember putting on scrubs, going toward the operating room, and then being told to wait outside until they called me.

I was about to kick the door down myself to get some answers when I finally got the call to come back. I took a quick glance around the room and saw a team of doctors standing around my wife's body. I saw a few nurses standing beside a table and an anesthesiologist standing by my wife's head. Then I noticed Alicia, lying on her back with a curtain drawn across her neck, blocking the view of what was taking place, and her arms were outstretched with her wrists tied down to the bed. She was shaking uncontrollably.

I pulled up a stool next to her and tried to think of something to say. I knew the events of the next few minutes were going to forever change our lives, either for the better or the worse. I trusted our doctor, but more importantly we both had come to fully trust the sovereignty of God, and we knew that nothing would happen that God had not already planned.

The silence was broken when the doctor said, "Wow, she *does* have a lot of hair." Within minutes, we could hear her crying, which I am convinced is the only time in the life of a baby that parents enjoy hearing them cry. And then at 8:57 p.m., Dr. Warren lifted up Reagan McKenzie Mann and let us take our first look at our baby girl.

Two days before her birth, the doctors estimated that she would weigh over six pounds when she was delivered, which explains my confusion when I looked at the reading on the scale they laid her on. The digital reading showed 4.145. I looked at the nurse and told her that I didn't know how to do conversions, but she only laughed and explained to me that Reagan weighed only four pounds and fifteen ounces. Then she showed me why we had to have the emergency C-section: Reagan had turned sideways in the birth canal and gotten stuck.

All the time spent on her side caused her to have what the doctor called a cone head. The right side of her skull was almost totally flat, and it came to a point at the top of the right side. We were told not to worry; apparently that is fairly common and corrects itself within forty-eight hours. Nevertheless I made sure we had a hat on her cone head before any of the family got to come back and see her.

In the morning, her skull looked almost totally normal, but just to be sure the pediatrician ordered X-rays of her skull. We had so many visitors coming by that day, and Alicia and I were enjoying ourselves and taking pictures of the baby when a new doctor came in. She explained to us that the X-rays from Reagan's skull had come back abnormal. What a party pooper!

They had to take Reagan to the Neonatal Intensive Care Unit (NICU) where a CT scan had already been ordered for her. We already knew the NICU rules: only two visitors at a time, one of which had to be a parent. Most people don't even get to hold their children in that unit.

The doctor was amazed by what she saw on the X-rays. Babies typically have either one or two "soft spots" on their heads, known medically as posterior and anterior fontanels. Reagan, however, only had one soft spot. The problem was that the soft spot covered the length of her skull from her forehead all the way down to the bottom of her head. It was almost as if she had two skull halves that never came together in the middle. I know it is a weird comparison, but the bone formation resembled a bald man that only has hair on the sides of his head. Furthermore, the X-rays appeared as if her brain may have penetrated part of the gap in her skull.

She took Reagan away and said that they would let us know when we could go down and see her. I had mixed feelings that evening. Part of me was terrified; my stomach dropped, and I felt as if my knees would give out on me. But I also had a calm feeling come over me. Maybe this is what the Bible refers to as a peace that passes understanding. It was as if the Lord was telling me that he had given us Reagan against all odds and that this was just one more obstacle that we would have to wait out.

While that was going on, Alicia was recovering physically from her surgery. She was understandably exhausted from the events of the preceding few days, but she was otherwise stable. Her blood pressure and kidney function were still being monitored, and the doctors were making sure that everything was under control.

That night we got to see our daughter again. As per NICU rules, we scrubbed our hands for two minutes in a little room before we entered the area where the babies were. We walked past several other babies before we got to Reagan; we tried not to look at them out of respect to the parents, but there were just some staggering sights there. Then we came to Reagan's bed, which may have been the most difficult part of the entire pregnancy and delivery process.

She was swaddled in a blanket and wearing a wool cap. Her left foot was attached by cords to a machine that monitored her vital statistics, like her heart rate, blood pressure, and respirations. She had an IV inserted into her left hand, and the port was so large that the doctors had to wrap it around her entire arm, which made her unable to bend her left arm. Her right hand was bruised where there had been an unsuccessful attempt to insert an IV there. There was also a feeding tube down her nose that went into her stomach.

Although she wasn't in an incubator that first night, she was two days later. That was even more unsettling because she hadn't been in one, and then the first time we saw her in it we couldn't find her nurse to explain to us why she had been placed in it. We finally found someone who was able to tell us that during the night her temperature had dropped below what was desired so she was incubated to get her body temperature back up.

Because of the CT scans that were run on consecutive days, Reagan was not allowed to eat beyond what was administered intravenously. Because of this, she was three days old the first time someone attempted to feed her with a bottle. She lost crucial training time for eating habits, so it took a while for her to learn how to eat. Any time the nurses could not get her to take as much as they wanted her to, the balance of the bottle was put down her feeding tube. To me, that only delayed the process of learning how to eat.

Reagan made progress over the next four days, and it finally looked as if she might be allowed to go home. We were told that if the nurse could watch us give her an entire bottle then she would be discharged. At that time, she was supposed to take forty cc's of formula (just over an ounce) at every feeding, which we were able to give her. Before she could be released, Alicia and I had to take an infant CPR class and take a test over what we had learned. While all of that was going on, the nurse tried to feed her again and was only able to give her thirty-six cc's instead of forty, which is only a few drops less. The verdict was she had to stay another night in the NICU.

The situation with her skull was still a mystery though. We met with a geneticist to try to assess whether any hereditary factors may have contributed to this rare case. We were each asked questions about our family's history, and the doctor told us he was going to send a

DVD of the X-rays to a bone specialist in Germany who was considered to be one of the leading doctors in his field in the entire world.

In the morning, Reagan took forty cc's and was discharged. We finally got to take our baby home and begin the process of parenthood. Things were going pretty well, but when she was five weeks old, we got a letter from the geneticist saying he had heard back from the doctor in Germany. That doctor had a team of other doctors brainstorming with him since he had never seen anything like her condition.

What they had feared was osteogenesis imperfecta (imperfect bone formation) didn't pan out. If that had been the case, then there would be fractures or breaks throughout her body, but the X-rays ruled that out. They decided they would categorize it as delayed ossification, hoping that in time the bones would fully develop to the point of normalcy.

At the time of this writing, Reagan will be fifteen months old this week, and she barely weighs seventeen pounds. She has been to a hematologist, oncologist, and endocrinologist, and no one can find a reason why she is so small. In fact, she is not even on the growth curve chart, which means she is in the bottom 3 percent in weight, skull circumference, and length, yet she is able to function in every way that a child her age is supposed to.

Her skull is almost totally normal though; that doctor from Germany came all the way to our house in Adamsburg, South Carolina, which is a city that makes Mayberry look like my hometown of Orlando. The doctor studied her, and he concluded that this was just one of those unexplainable things, and he got our permission to use her in his case studies.

My purpose for opening the book this way is to establish the fact that I have been there. I know the pain of miscarriage all too well, and even worse, I know the pain of trying to come to grips with the idea of never having your own biological children. This book is not written by some psychologist getting paid $200 an hour to listen to your hurts. I have been there with my wife, I know the hurts, and I have found healing. In essence, I am one beggar trying to show other beggars where to find food.

My other purpose for opening with this chapter is to give hope. Maybe you have given up on the idea of having your own children. Maybe, like me, you are viewing infertility as your lot in life. If that is where you find yourself, then let me share with you the same advice that one of our doctors in Orlando shared with us: as long as you are physically and emotionally able to handle it, then keep trying. I know people that have spent years, even *decades*, in futile attempts to have children before the Lord gave them the desire of their heart.

I am not trying to give you false hope, for since the Lord is the giver of life, this is genuine hope. Keep your trust in God, and don't give up!

It's Not Your Fault

The most natural human instinct after the loss of a child is for the parents to blame themselves. While this is more often seen with the mothers instead of with the fathers, many men will become slaves to their own guilt as well.

Many women who have miscarried will go back and try to think of anything that they may have done wrong during their pregnancy. Things will begin to come back to her mind—things she may have done weeks or months earlier. She may find herself thinking, *If only I had exercised more* or *If only I had not exercised so much.* She may begin to wonder about things like, *Was my nail polish remover too strong?* or *Did this happen because I inhaled the fumes from cleaning supplies?*

On and on the list could go of possible things that may have seemingly led to this event. The truth is, though, that ninety-nine times out of a hundred none of those things would have been factors. There are plenty of documented cases of women who smoked cigarettes and drank alcohol throughout an entire pregnancy and the baby turned out to be just fine.

Let me pause and remind the reader that I am not a medical doctor. This is by no means a defense of alcohol or nicotine usage during pregnancy; neither is it a green light to use cleaning chemicals or nail polish remover. Those have the potential to do harm, although mostly only in overexposure, but there is sufficient evidence that a pregnant woman *can be* exposed to those things and have no negative effects.

In most situations in which there has been a miscarriage, the cause will forever be unknown. Once a couple has experienced several, there may be some genetic testing done, or sometimes the doctor can find an explanation as to what occurred. But usually this is just chalked up as an unexplained phenomenon. The point is, don't blame yourself.

Assuming that the mother was not a chain smoker or intentionally overly exposed to harmful chemicals, there is no way to place the blame on anything that she might have done. Give yourself a break; you have too many other emotions going on right now to beat yourself (or your spouse) up.

If you have lost a child to SIDS, I hope you have heard by now that there will never be a known reason for why that happened. Doctors come to the conclusion of SIDS when there is no other explanation; this means that no one is placing the blame on you, so you should not place it on yourself.

Still other people may look to place the blame on some past event in their life. In essence, they are asking, "Is God punishing me?" Many people begin to retrace their steps to see if there was some sin, some offense that may have caused God to pour out his wrath in this way. Please hear me out: this thought should not be ruled out; however, I believe that it is usually not the case.

I often tell people that God is not in the business of what I like to call "secret discipline." By this I mean that if God were to punish a person, he would let them know why and what they did. The reason for this is that God only punishes us to make us better people. God is not a playground bully looking for some nerd to pick on; no, his punishment is always for our benefit. In Jeremiah 29 God tells the prophet Jeremiah that he will be punishing the nation of Israel because of their rebellion, but in the eleventh verse of that chapter God gives Jeremiah a promise to cling to. He said that his plans were to give Israel peace, not evil, and to give them a future and a hope.

God's desire is for our sanctification, which is just a fancy churchy way of saying that God wants us to be holy or set apart from the world. Whenever we as Christians fail at this, we should expect God's punishment, which we invited into our lives through our sin.

But God is not in the business of secret discipline. Just imagine a father walking into the room of his teenage son and saying, "You're grounded. No TV, no computer, no cell phone, and give me the keys."

"But dad, what did I do?" would be the son's reply.

Now imagine this answer from the father: "None of your business!" That is not punishment; it is torture.

In the same way, what if a mother came in to her daughter's room and just started spanking her. "What did I do wrong?"

"I'm not telling you!" That is not discipline; it is abuse.

Punishment is always done for the benefit of the one being punished. If you don't like those examples, let me use another illustration. When a person is house breaking a dog, there is usually a rolled up newspaper or some other form of punishment involved whenever the dog leaves his owners a surprise on the carpet. This is not done out of hatred for the dog. The dog owner has a goal in mind, and he knows that this form of correction will bring about the desired results.

When God punishes a person, his Holy Spirit will let the person know what they did wrong. If this did not happen, then how would the person learn from his mistake? If he didn't know where he erred, it would just be a matter of time until he committed the same offense again and receive more punishment for it. This would not be fair, and God's goal of holy living would not be achieved.

For this reason, I believe that God *might* use the loss of a child as a form of punishment but *only if he lets the person know what they did wrong*. There are several undeniable occurrences in the Bible in which a child was lost or a woman became infertile as a punishment for sin, but in each of those situations, the people were told by God why it was happening, and it only followed either severe rebellion or serious offences. Consider Michal, who became barren after she criticized David for dancing before the Lord (2 Samuel 6:23), and Bathsheba, who lost the son she conceived in adultery (2 Samuel 12:19).

In Genesis 20, God temporarily made all the women of the house of Abimelech infertile because Abimielech tried to take a married woman as one of his wives, but as soon as the Lord revealed his sin to him, he repented; then Abimelech's wife and all his female servants bore children.

It should be noted that while there are certain biblical cases in which the Lord did see fit to carry out his righteous judgment in this fashion, there are far more cases in which he did the opposite. Women who for so long were labeled as being barren were blessed by the Lord and given children. Consider the testimonies of Sarah (Genesis 21:2-3), Rebekah (Genesis 25:21), Rachel (Genesis 30:22-24), the unnamed mother of Samson (Judges 13:1-3), and Hannah (1 Samuel 1:27).

So if God has not revealed some infraction on your part that led to tragedy, stop blaming yourself. If he has revealed something to you, repent of the sin, apologize to God, and pray that he gives you another chance.

I want to say one thing to the people reading this who are not Christians. God's goal for your life is sanctification, but it is in a different sense than it is with those who are Christians. Sanctification is both positional and progressive. It is positional in the fact that you have to change your position by becoming a follower of Christ (you change from being a sinner to being a saint). It is progressive in that you spend the rest of your life becoming more like Christ by becoming set apart.

So God's goal for you is your sanctification, but right now he wants you to have a positional sanctification. Turn from your sins, and give your life to Christ right now. He is calling out to you. In Matthew 11:28 Jesus beckons, "Come unto me." But the reason that I mention all of this is that I want you to know that God does not punish the unbeliever like he punishes the believer. You probably did not lose a child as the result of the punishment for sin because God is not molding you like he does those who call him Lord.

This does not mean that you should live your life apart from Christ to escape punishment, for that will only seal your eternal punishment. God punishes his children on this earth during this life so that we will live right and not face an eternal punishment. But the ones who reject him may live a life free from any punishment on this earth but spend eternity being punished for living their life apart from Jesus Christ.

When Does a Life Become a Life?

One of the most debated questions of our time is over the issue of the unborn: When does a life become a life? There are those who hold to the idea that a baby is not an actual human life until he takes his first breath outside the womb without the aid of his mother. There is another camp, usually in Christian circles, that passionately believes that a human life is created at conception, from the time that a zygote (fertilized egg) is formed. There are also people in the middle, found on all points of a timeline, who cite that a fetus becomes a life after the formation of the heart, or the lungs, or when he becomes shaped like a human.

This is a very difficult question to answer since the babies can't answer when we question. No one can think back to the time when they were in that gestation period themselves, leaving each of us unable to answer the question from personal experience.

One way to answer the question is to look at the possible answers and use the process of elimination. Is the answer to the question that a baby is not a human life until birth? If that were the case, then how do we reconcile the fact that some babies are born full term at forty weeks while others are born prematurely as early as twenty-four weeks? That fortieth week cannot be the finishing touch on forming a life if a baby is considered viable outside the womb at twenty-four weeks.

In order for a grown man to be considered to be alive, he would need a beating heart, working lungs, and brain activity. Those are all accounted for inside the womb, so by common sense standards, it does not take birth to create a life.

A person could watch a baby on the screen of an ultrasound machine and observe a functioning life. One could see movement, thumb sucking, yawning, a beating heart, expanding lungs, opening and closing of the eyes and mouth, and so on. Babies can even show personality at this stage. It would be hard to observe all of this and not come to the conclusion that this fetus is, in fact, very much alive.

Is the answer to the question found somewhere on a timeline between conception and birth? One could almost make the case that the baby is not a life until after the thirty-seventh week when the lungs become mature. However, a baby could be born thirteen weeks prior to the full development of the lungs and still survive with the help of an incubator and respirator. We do not consider an adult to have ceased from being a life just because he requires the aid of a respirator to breathe, so we should not with babies either.

Also important on the timeline is a functioning heart, which can be found as early as twenty-two *days* after conception. For a baby to be miscarried or aborted after that point requires a heart to stop beating. It is hard to believe that anything with a beating heart is not a life. Even so, doctors put pacemakers in people all the time. A pacemaker is a device that makes the heart beat, which means that the natural heart is not beating; no one would consider an adult with a pacemaker to not be a life because his own heart doesn't beat.

Science also shows us that as early as six weeks after conception there are identifiable brain waves in this new life. Since the majority of abortions are performed after the ninth week, this requires stopping a beating heart and functioning brain.

At which point on this timeline would you say that a baby becomes an actual life?

- Day 1—fertilization
- Day 6—embryo implants in the uterus
- Day 22—a heart pumps the baby's own blood
- Week 3—spinal column, nervous system, liver, and kidneys forming
- Week 4—the baby is 10,000 times larger than it was at conception
- Week 5—eyes, hands, and legs are developing
- Week 6—brain waves are noticeable; mouth, lips, and fingernails are forming
- Week 7—eye lids, toes, and nose are forming; he is swimming and kicking

- Week 8—every organ is in place; cartilage is turning into bone; he has unique fingerprints and he can hear
- Weeks 9-10—teeth are developing in the gums; he can hiccup
- Weeks 11-12—he can urinate and "practices breathing"; he has a full skeletal structure
- Week 12—vocal chords are complete
- Week 14—the heart pumps several quarts of blood per day
- Week 15—he has all his taste buds
- Month 4—his bone marrow is forming and he weighs half a pound

This timeline shows that there is never one clear point where anyone can definitively say that there is a human life. What is more likely then is that all of the ingredients for life are present at conception and develop over time until the God-ordained time of birth.

There was a picture that was circulated several years ago from a doctor who performed surgery on a baby that was still in the mother's womb. Tests revealed that the baby was going to have spina bifida and an operation was needed prior to delivery. In surgery, the womb was removed from the mother and cut open so that the doctor could operate on the baby. A photograph was taken when the baby extended a tiny arm out of the womb and grabbed the doctor's finger.

To many people, that was just a fetus, a far cry from a human life. How could a person conclude that this was not yet a life after watching him behave as if he were? Sadly, the doctor who performed that operation also performs abortions, and he was unchanged by the miracle of life he witnessed that day in the OR.

Does life begin at conception? So far science cannot tell us. Since life has to begin sometime before birth, why not err on the safe side and consider the possibility that life begins at conception.

One thing to consider is the fact that a zygote is genetically complete, containing all forty-six chromosomes that a person needs, with even the baby's gender, hair and eye color, and height already determined. Thus at the very second of conception all the genetic makeup of a human life is present and accounted for. This new life that is formed has unique DNA; no one before or after him will ever have the same genetic makeup, yet there are many who would like us to believe that fetuses are common and just a dime a dozen.

Some will argue that crushing an acorn is not the same as chopping down a tree, using the acorn to represent the baby and the tree to represent an adult. They make the case that an acorn is not a tree but just a potential tree. An acorn is not just a *potential* tree though; it is a tree in its earliest form. In the same way, a baby is not just a potential human life; it is life in the earliest form. To crush an acorn is to prevent a mighty oak tree from growing, and to terminate a baby's development is to prevent a life from growing.

Earlier I mentioned that at conception all the ingredients for life are present and that they require time to develop. Many supporters of abortion will use this logic against the pro-life crowd saying that if it has to develop into a life, then it is not a life. To use their terminology: If A *has to develop* into B, then A *is not* B.

This sounds good, but it is easily refuted. No one denies the fact that a born baby is a life, and that baby is obviously different than his adult counterpart. What accounts for the difference between the two? The adult was a baby who continued to develop over time into an adult.

If a person killed a six-month-old baby, he has committed murder; he prevented the baby from developing into an adult. No one would ever make the case that it is not murder because the six-month-old had not developed into an adult yet. In the same way, a fetus is a developing baby, which is a developing toddler, which is a developing child, which is a developing teenager, which is a developing adult. To stop the process at any point is to stop a life.

Our own judicial system views an unborn baby as a life. If a drunk driver hit and kills a pregnant woman with his car, he can be found guilty of a double murder or of double manslaughter (even if this woman were on her way to legally abort her baby).

More important than what science teaches and what the judicial system acknowledges is what the Bible tells us. Can this two-thousand-year-old book answer the question of when a baby becomes a life?

While the Bible was not written to be a history or science book, everything the Bible says about history and science is accurate. Critics of the Bible have tried for years to disprove its validity by attempting to find an error in some of the ancient cities and characters the Bible mentions, but for centuries these efforts have all been made in vain.

In the same way, the Bible has always been accurate on scientific measures as well; for example, thousands of years before science could prove the earth was not flat, the Bible already made the case for a round earth (Job 26:7, Isaiah 40:21-22, Proverbs 8:27).

This is a necessary context when exploring what the Bible has to say about the formation of a human life. Even if the majority opinion in the world today is that life does not begin until birth (hypothetically, of course), if the Bible speaks otherwise, then the majority opinion is simply wrong. When the majority opinion was that Christopher Columbus would sail off the edge of a flat earth and the Bible taught that the earth is round, the majority opinion was wrong. So let's take a look at what the Bible says about when a life becomes a life.

The psalmist of Psalm 71:6 said that he would praise the Lord because the Lord protected him in the womb and delivered him out of it. Psalm 139:13 says that the Lord "covered me" in the womb. The expression "covered me" means to weave together. The New International Version translates it this way: "You knit me together in my mother's womb."

In Isaiah 44:2, God tells Israel not to fear because God "formed [them] in the womb" and he would continue to protect them. Just twenty-two verses later, God reminds them again that he formed them in the womb. These verses show that God is intimately aware of those living in the womb of the mother.

In Isaiah 49:1 and 5, Isaiah proclaims that God formed him in the womb and that God chose him and called his name. These verses show that what is in the womb is not some random, lifeless glob; this is a unique person whom God is interested in.

In Jeremiah 1:5, God tells Jeremiah that he sanctified him as a prophet before he came out of the womb and that God knew him before he formed him in the womb. This verse shows that not only did God know him in the womb, he knew him before *he formed him in the womb*. As a baby continues to form in the womb, God is actively at work doing the forming.

In the New Testament, in Luke 1:15, the parents of John the Baptist were told that their son would be filled with the Holy Ghost in his mother's womb. Since the Holy Ghost would not indwell within something that was not yet a life, this verse shows that John was alive in the womb even before his birth. In verse forty-one of the same chapter, John was dancing for joy in his mother's womb when Mary told her cousin that she was pregnant with Jesus.

Furthermore, Zechariah 12:1 says that the Lord forms the spirit of man within him. The Bible does not specifically say that this is done at the moment of conception, but it certainly is not done after birth. When else would this be done if not at conception?

So the Bible makes it very clear that it is not the action of a baby exiting the birth canal that creates a life. Before birth, even before conception, the Bible says that God had intimate knowledge with and was actively involved in the lives of these babies. The point is, an unborn baby is a life, even if the only person to know him was God.

Why is this an important question to answer? It goes far beyond politics. The previous section shows that the child you may have lost was knit together by God even though he never made it to birth. The first step in finding healing is actually to understand the fact that a lost baby was a human life. Personally I believe that the three miscarriages we had resulted in the death of three children. Without the miscarriages, then those babies would have been ours to raise.

Initially my wife found comfort in trying to convince herself that those were never babies; it was easier to believe the myth that this was just a glob of tissue. In the end, she came to terms with the fact that she had conceived human life but under the sovereignty of God was not permitted to raise them.

Many people will wonder what was actually developing inside them during a pregnancy, especially if the baby was lost during the first trimester. I am a firm believer that what was developing was a human, no matter how small. If, then, there was a human life that is no longer here, then it must have gone somewhere.

Does the unborn baby live on, or does it simply cease to exist? Where does he go? Did my baby really go to heaven? Will I get to see him again, and if so, what will he look like?

Is My Baby Really in Heaven?

The Bible is very clear that both heaven and hell are real places. According to God's Word, every person has an appointment with death, after which we will all be judged (Hebrews 9:27). There are only two options at this point: some will be welcomed into heaven, while others are sent to their place of eternal punishment in the lake of fire.

Before I go on, though, I must stress the fact that there is no middle ground. One would search the Bible in vain for any mention of a so-called purgatory or any other holding cell in between heaven and hell. This is important because each person must make sure that he knows he is ready to make it to heaven before his death.

Is Heaven Real?

Most surveys would show us that the majority of Americans believe that heaven is a real place. This is only natural—who would not want to believe that they would go to heaven when they die? But hoping for something good does not prove its reality.

How do we prove the existence of a place that we cannot visit or see? Science cannot prove that there is a heaven. No matter how far NASA is able to explore, they will never come upon the pearly gates.

Like most aspects of Christianity, the concept of heaven is something that must be believed purely in faith. The Bible gives us a few glimpses of what we can expect to see in heaven, but even God's Word does little to exhaust the topic. There are a few passages in Revelation 21-22 that offer a few descriptions of what heaven will be like after the great tribulation, but the best sentence to sum up heaven is found in 1 Corinthians 2:9: "Eye hath not seen, nor ear heard, neither have entered into the heart of man, the things which God hath prepared for them that love Him."

In essence, there is no way for a human to describe the beauty of heaven.

But even beyond any description of heaven is the matter-of-fact statement about its existence in the first sentence of the Bible: "In the beginning God created the heavens and the earth" (Genesis 1:1). The Bible teaches that God created everything, and common sense should always affirm this to be true.

This is not a work to disprove the *theory* of evolution, but just think about what that theory teaches. Evolution can be summed up in one sentence: First there was nothing, and then it exploded. Where did the two molecules that collided come from? After a hundred and fifty years, they still do not have an answer.

And yet in that explosion all matter in the universe was sent spinning, randomly forming the most complex entities. Think about the human eye, brain, or nervous system. We are supposed to believe that this is all the result of random chance? That is like saying that a tornado went through a junkyard, and after it left, there was a Boeing 747 where all the junk used to be. No matter how many billions of years it took, a tornado never could pull off a task like that.

The point is that we obviously were created. If we were created, there has to be a Creator. If there is a Creator, he deserves to be worshipped as God. If he is God, then he must also be Lord, and if he is Lord, then he will be our judge. So to eliminate the necessity to obey the Lord and answer to a judge, scientists promote this improvable theory called evolution.

We obviously were created by a Creator who is the God of the universe. He is the God of the Bible, and the Bible says that God created a place called heaven where *some* people will go when they die.

How Does a Person Make It to Heaven?

The Bible is very clear about the fact that a person cannot earn the right to enter heaven. Romans 3:23 tells us that all of us have sinned (literally "missed the mark") and fallen short of God's standard, which is perfection. If you only sinned one time in your entire life, that one sin still has caused you to miss the mark. Upon your death, that sin will eternally separate you from God and send you to hell.

While Romans 3:23 convicts us of our sin, Romans 6:23 presents the case for our acquittal. That verse says that the punishment for our sins is death, but God offers us a gift of eternal life through Jesus Christ our Lord.

A gift is something that is unearned; you don't have to do enough good deeds for your parents to give you a birthday present. It is the same way with this gift from God. Your good deeds do not guarantee any special treatment from God.

But just as with any other gift, you still have to act to make it your own. This is where a lot of people get off the path. If your parents gave you a birthday present and you just stared at it and never moved, you have not received the gift. You can acknowledge that it is there, you can believe it is there, and you can even love it, but unless that belief leads you to action, you have not received the gift.

The gift must be received; you have to reach out and grab it. The gift from God must be received as well. Romans 10:13 says that anyone who calls on the name of the Lord will be saved. Too many people have interpreted this verse to say, "Whoever says a prayer will be saved" or "Whoever asks Jesus into their heart will be saved." That just simply is not the biblical formula.

To call upon the Lord is not a one-time prayer that is offered asking for salvation. Instead, this verse is telling us that we have to put our faith in action. A mere belief in God does not bring salvation; the Bible says that even the demons believe in God and tremble with fear (James 2:19). Your belief in God has to lead to a changed heart and subsequently a changed life.

Jesus said if you love him, then you would keep his commandments (John 14:15), yet many people in

American churches today do not keep God's commandments. The average person thinks he is doing a pretty good job because he doesn't murder or cheat on his spouse, but there is more to it than that.

If you have ever told a lie, you have broken a commandment. If you have ever taken something that was not yours, you have broken a commandment. If you have ever used God's holy name in an unholy way, you have broken a commandment (blasphemy). Jesus even took two of the commandments a step further and said that if you are angry with someone without a reason or if you look at another person lustfully, then you have committed murder and adultery respectively. To top it all off, the Bible says that if you have broken *just one* of the commandments, then you are guilty of breaking *all* of the commandments (James 2:10).

Please know that I am not saying you can work your way to heaven. No amount of good works can ever compensate for the amount of evil works we continually commit. Good works are not required *for* salvation, but good works are required *from* salvation. If you truly love the Lord, you would rightly view works as worship.

So then the test to see if you really are a Christian is not to ask yourself if you love God, if God loves you, or if you have prayed some prayer. One true test is to see if you keep God's commandments. And remember, you cannot be a Christian without having good works as evidence in your life.

Another way to test yourself is to examine your relationship with Christ. *There is no salvation apart from a relationship with Jesus.* It is not just belief in God plus keeping his commandments that will save you; there has to be one-on-one time with the Master. Consider the verdict from Jesus in Matthew 7:23. At their judgment, Jesus says the majority of the people will try to impress him with a list of all the good things they accomplished in life, but Jesus will sentence them to the fate they chose over him: everlasting punishment in the lake of fire.

These people do not go to hell because they were axe murderers or rapists. They seem like genuinely good people, but it is not good people that make it to heaven; it is godly people. In this verse, Jesus explains that he never knew them, which is an expression that refers to a deep, intimate relationship between husband and wife. This expression is not referring to sexual intimacy but the joining of mind and spirit in the relationship that is the most intimate way two people can know each other.

Do you know Jesus that way? This intimate knowledge comes through time spent in Bible study and seeking God through prayer. Too many people call themselves Christians on Sunday yet never touch a Bible from Monday through Saturday, and their only prayer time is fifteen seconds before a meal or asking God for some request. You must have an actual relationship with Jesus in order to call yourself his child.

A key factor in salvation is repentance, which has been misinterpreted as asking for forgiveness or simply saying you are sorry for something. The actual definition of repentance involves a turning away. This means that a person will turn from an old way of life and turn toward following Christ, leaving behind old sins and an old lifestyle. When a person repents, he will not find himself asking for forgiveness for the same sins over and over again; he will turn away from that sin and keep the commandments of Christ.

If you have never repented, put your faith in Jesus, started a real relationship with Jesus, or if you do not have the evidence of good works in your life, you need to make some changes right now in order to become a Christian. Do not let another minute go by; stop right now and commit your life to Christ. He is waiting for you.

The Age of Accountability

This now brings us to a difficult question. Some readers are now beginning to realize that their child never repented, never had a relationship with Christ, never displayed good works, and never put his faith in Jesus. *Is my baby really in heaven?*

I can confidently answer this question with a yes. I believe that there is grace that covers people until they are at a place where they can make a conscious decision between right and wrong. This idea has become known as the "age of accountability."

There is not one magic number, no certain age where a person becomes accountable. This is different for each person. One five-year-old may not be able to comprehend the idea of living in obedience to a higher power while another five-year-old may quickly understand it. On the other hand, a thirty-five-year-old man with a mental handicap may still not be quite ready to grasp such a concept.

Nowhere in the Bible can the phrase "age of accountability" be found. In fact, there is no language even close to that phrase. That does not discredit the concept, though, for there are several people in God's Word that give us an insight into this truth.

Abraham

Abraham, the father of Israel, found himself haggling with God over the destruction of Sodom. God told Abraham that he was going to destroy the city because of their sexual perversion—namely, rampant homosexuality (Genesis 18)—and Abraham tried to persuade God to spare the city if he could find fifty righteous people living there. Sadly, there were not fifty righteous people in the entire city; Abraham continued to try to talk God into saving the city if there forty-five righteous people, then forty, then thirty, then twenty, and then ten. There were not even found ten righteous people, so the Lord destroyed that wicked city with fire.

Abraham posed a rhetorical question. In Genesis 18:25, Abraham asked the Lord, "Shall not the Judge of all the earth do right?"

The first thing that we need to realize is that God is the judge of all the earth and he will do what is right. No one gets to heaven unless they get through Judge Jesus, and the Bible tells us that he will do what is right. Second Corinthians 5:10 says we will all stand before the judgment seat of Christ and there we will receive either good or bad judgment, according to the choices we made in life.

It is a dangerous game when a person starts to interpret the Bible based on what they think or feel may be right, but I also am a firm believer that the closer a Christian gets to the Father through prayer and Bible study, the more he will be able to know, not guess, what God is like. The Bible teaches that if a person will draw close to God, then God will draw close to him (James 4:8), which will allow that person to know God more.

With the knowledge that God will do what is right, a spiritually deep person can easily come to the conclusion that Jesus the judge would not hold innocent children accountable for his laws before they can mentally comprehend them. Those of us who have lost children should rest easy with the knowledge that the judge of all the earth will do what is right with our children.

Moses

The next passage comes from the Old Testament law that Moses gave to the children of Israel. In those days, an animal sacrifice was required for the forgiveness of sins, and each person was responsible for making his own sacrifice. The only exception to that rule was the children who were not old enough to make their own sacrifice or to even understand the purpose of forgiveness. These children were covered by the sacrifices of their parents (Exodus 30:14).

A similar situation occurred when it came time for the children of Israel to enter the promised land. Follow this story of Israel's early history:

For years Israel had been held as slaves in Egypt until God appointed Moses to lead them to freedom. Even though God used a series of miracles to lead them out of captivity (ten plagues, crossing the Red Sea, manna from heaven, etc.), the Israelites continually complained and even wished that they were still slaves in Egypt.

God patiently tolerated their complaining, but eventually punishment had to come.

After they left Egypt, the Israelites were supposed to go to the promised land, which is modern-day Israel. But because of their constant complaining, God issued judgment that they would no longer be allowed to enter this new land. They would have to wander in the wilderness for the remainder of their lives.

The only ones who were allowed to enter the promised land were the ones who were nineteen years old and younger at the time of this punishment. Forty years later, when the last of the older generation had died off, this new generation could move in and possess their new land.

Why were the younger ones allowed to live? Why were they not punished for their sin? The answer is found in Deuteronomy 1:39, where God said that these little ones had no knowledge between good and evil. This is important: when all of humanity was judged guilty because of their sin, the children who were not capable of understanding the difference between right and wrong were not held accountable. The judge of all the earth will do what is right with them.

David

Also one must consider the situation with King David. David, who was a married man, was the king of Israel. During a time of war when the king was supposed to be near the action, David was at home admiring the wife of another man.

This woman's name was Bathsheba, and she was the wife of Uriah, one of the king's soldiers. In a classic case of irony, David spied on Bathsheba while she was taking a bath. David lusted after her in his heart and then made the decision to consummate his lust. With her husband being away at war, David thought he could easily get away with this one-night stand. His plan blew up in his face when Bathsheba brought him the news that she was pregnant.

David had to act quickly to keep himself from getting caught in adultery, so he gave the order for Uriah to come home for a night. The idea was that Uriah would sleep with his wife and think that the child she conceived was his. Much to David's surprise the next morning, Uriah had refused to sleep with his wife since that would not have been fair to his fellow soldiers who were still serving.

David realized that his only two options at that point were to come clean with his affair or kill Uriah. In a decision that would forever alter David's life, the king gave the order for Uriah to be sent to the front lines and then for the army to retreat. The plan worked for David, as Uriah was killed from behind during the retreat.

This was a seeming win-win situation for David; Uriah was now out of the picture, and David could appear to be honorable by taking Bathsheba as his wife (in those days, it was not uncommon for a man, especially a king, to have multiple wives). This way he could marry Bathsheba and everyone would assume that the child was conceived after their marriage.

Unbeknownst to David, God had revealed this extra-marital relationship to the prophet Nathan. Nathan confronted the king with his sin, and David repented. God spared David's life despite his iniquity, and he let him remain king, but his punishment was far from light. Among other things, God would not allow the child that Bathsheba delivered to live any longer.

When the news was brought to David that his youngest child had indeed died, David's sorrow was great. His words spoken during his grief provide more profound evidence for an age of accountability than arguably any other words recorded in the entire Bible. In 2 Samuel 12:23, David said of his son, "Can I bring him back again? I shall go to him, but he shall not return to me."

These are not just the words of a mourning father; every word written in the Bible was recorded through the hands of men but was breathed by the Spirit of God (2 Timothy 3:16). David knew that no amount of praying or fasting would bring his son back from the grave, but he was confident in the fact that he would one day go to see his son. The two would someday be reunited in the presence of God.

Paul

The Apostle Paul never lost a child, or even had a child for that matter, but he gives us some insight into the accountability of a child. We just looked at David's experience with his child; now we will look at Paul's experience as a child.

In his letter to the Romans, Paul spoke of a time when he was "without the law." Since Paul learned God's laws at a young age according to Acts 22, the time he was without the law must have been when he was a child. In Paul's letter, he said, "For I was alive without the law once, but when the commandment came, sin revived, and I died. And the commandment, which was ordained to life, I found to be unto death" (Romans 7:9-10).

Isolated from its context, these verses might not make much sense. Please allow me to explain. Paul is describing his own journey into an age of accountability. When he was a young child who didn't know the law, he was alive, but when the commandment came, he gained knowledge of what is right and wrong. Sin revived—that is, he saw sin for what it really was—and he died. This was not a physical death but a death to self, the kind of self-denial that Jesus calls for when a person begins to live his life in accordance with God's Word.

To sum up what the apostle was saying, there was a time in his life when he was too young to understand God's law, but after he was able to comprehend it, he died to himself and yet was born into a new life with Christ. If Paul had died prior to being able to understand the law, I believe he would have been found not guilty at his judgment.

Finally, Paul, like Abraham before him, recognized the fact that the Lord is the judge of all the earth. In his first letter to Timothy, Paul said that the Lord would serve as judge when he returns. It is encouraging to read both Old and New Testament saints teaching that there is a just judge that will do what is right with our children.

Other Verses

We have been looking at the lives of individuals in the Scriptures, but now we will look at individual Scriptures. I will not spend time setting up the background for these verses, but the biblical truth about a child's accountability can still be clearly seen. I encourage the reader to look these verses up and read them in their context.

Isaiah 7:16: "For before the child shall know to refuse the evil and choose the good..." This verse shows that children are simply unable to choose between right and wrong until they reach a certain point.

Romans 9:11: "For the children being not yet born, neither having done any good or evil..." This verse establishes the fact that unborn children have committed no evil and thus cannot be viewed as guilty before God.

Ezekiel 28:15: "Thou wast perfect in thy ways from the day that thou wast created, till iniquity was found in thee." This was God's assessment of the king of Tyre. He was perfect for a time after his creation.

Zechariah 12:1: "[God forms] the spirit of man within him." If God forms a baby's spirit inside him, would God form a sinful spirit? No. God forms a perfect spirit, just like with Adam and Eve, and one day that spirit will choose to sin on his own. An unborn baby has not made that choice.

Criticism for the Age of Accountability

This next section has been included because there are probably some readers who have dismissed the idea of an age of accountability based on some reasoning heard elsewhere. Critics of the age of accountability can present a persuasive case against such an idea, but their case can easily be refuted. Listed below are some of the criticisms that I have heard offered.

#1: The phrase "age of accountability" does not appear in the Bible.

The notion that something should be discredited simply because its exact wording does not appear in the Bible is ludicrous. There are countless biblical concepts that do not necessarily appear in the Bible the way that we might want them to, but with a little bit of looking, these truths can be unlocked. The words *rapture* and *trinity* do not appear in the Bible, but they are almost universally accepted as Christian doctrine.

#2: What about the death of children in the Bible?

Some have tried to reason that if the Lord really loved children the way that Christians say he does, then why did children die in the Bible? For that matter, why do children die today?

The fact that children die physically does not change their eternal state. In fact, the Bible says there are two types of death: physical and spiritual. All people will face a physical death, and this is certainly no indication of disfavor from God. What is important is to make sure that after our physical death we do not suffer a spiritual death as well. Christians will only die once—that is, a physical death. The unsaved will find themselves spending eternity separated from God in the hell that is the lake of fire. This is the second death (Revelation 21:8).

What is important to know is that even though our children may have experienced a physical death, they will never have to worry about a spiritual death. Instead, they rest safely in the presence of Jesus.

#3: The age of accountability only applies to the children of Christians.

That just simply is not true. I have heard a number of Christians try to make this claim by saying that the children of Christian parents are "under the grace" of their parents. The Bible is very clear, however, that no one can get saved for another person. My parents' salvation cannot get me into heaven any more than some stranger's salvation could.

Also, in order to believe this claim to be true, one first presupposes the idea that the age of accountability itself must be true. With all the verses that have already been listed as proof of the age of accountability, the point has also been made that Jesus views these children as innocent. Their innocence is based on the mercy and grace of Jesus and their inability to discern between right and wrong, not on the condition of their parents' salvation.

With that knowledge in mind, when unsaved parents lose a baby, it may actually be because of the *mercy* of God. Two non-Christians parents rarely raise a child that becomes a Christian, so if their child is lost prior to reaching the age of accountability, then that child will go to heaven.

#4: The only way to heaven is through Jesus, and that rule applies to babies too.

There is a list of Bible verses that this camp will use to establish their case. They use Jesus's words from John 14:6: "I am the way, the truth, and the life. No man cometh unto the Father but by me." However, we have already examined the fact that Jesus is the judge of all the earth, and he will do what is right with these children. Remember, they never had the chance to make the choice to go through Jesus to get to the Father. In their innocence, I believe that Jesus will judge them not guilty.

Another verse they use is, ironically, from one of King David's prayers. However, one of David's prayers is the leading case *for* the age of accountability. In Psalm 51:5, David prayed, "Behold, I was shapen in iniquity, and in sin did my mother conceive me." They say this verse proves that each person is a sinner from conception. First of all, no, it doesn't. This verse simply proves *his mother's sin*, which has never been in question.

Second, even if a child were a sinner from conception, there is a world of theological difference between sin and sinning. The former refers to the sin problem that separates man from God, while the latter refers to the sins that people commit on a daily basis.

This comes back to the theological idea of original sin, which was brought about by Adam and Eve in the garden of Eden in Genesis 3. The Bible teaches that by one man (Adam) sin entered into the world (Romans 5:12), and the consequence of his sin is universal death because all people since Adam have sinned.

Romans 5 continues on to teach of another man (Jesus), known as the second Adam, who once and for all defeated death. By one man, sin entered into the world, and by one man, death was defeated (Romans 5:15).

When Jesus died on the cross, he died to satisfy the sin problem. In order to maintain his own holiness, God had to punish the sin of the world, so he poured out his wrath on his sinless Son, Jesus Christ. In so doing, God created the option for humanity to choose to accept this gift and become a child of God.

If that didn't make sense to you, maybe this will: Jesus's death took on sin in two ways. He fixed the sin problem once and for all and gave us power over *our* sins. Imagine a courtroom setting in which you are the guilty defendant and God is the judge. You have been found guilty and sentenced to death. But then (quite dramatically) the back doors swing open, and Jesus enters. He loudly proclaims, "Your Honor, he is guilty, but I want you to punish me instead."

The job of the judge is to punish the crime. In this scenario, the judge can do his job and the *sinner can go free.* That is how Jesus fixed the sin problem with his death on the cross. He gave God the opportunity to punish the sin while still entering into a relationship with an unholy person.

I said all that to make this point: even if a child were conceived in sin, he has committed no sins. His only sin problem was cured at Calvary by the shed blood of Jesus Christ. This is why I began this whole argument on the fundamental idea that Jesus is the judge of all the earth and he will do what is right.

So yes, it is true that no one gets to the Father except through Jesus, but these children are getting there through what Jesus has already done. For those of us who have reached an age where we are accountable for our own decisions, we have to make the choice for ourselves to go to Jesus for salvation. In our situation, Jesus has fixed the sin problem, but we have to do something about our sins. Babies have committed no sins.

Many times I have heard people say that babies are lying when they cry but then suddenly stop when their mother picks them up or they get their bottle. That is ridiculous! What do you expect that three-month-old to do? "Mother, I would be delighted if you would pick me up and give me my bottle please." Crying is a baby's language, and it is not deceitful.

Hopefully this has helped you come to the realization that children that are lost through miscarriage, abortion, SIDS, or anything else will spend eternity with their Father God in heaven. With that being established, the next question that usually arises is, What will my child look like in heaven?

What Will My Child Look Like in Heaven?

This is a question that the parents of a miscarried or aborted baby often find themselves wondering. The answer to the question is that we simply don't know for sure. There are two possible options that will be considered.

In heaven, these children could appear just as they were at the time they went to heaven. For example, a child miscarried at eight months may exist in heaven as a six-pound baby that is eighteen inches long, while a baby miscarried at eight weeks may exist in heaven being less than one inch long.

Another theory suggests that in heaven we will all have an apparent age comparable to the way that Adam and Eve were not born but created as young adults seemingly in their prime. For example, a baby lost at eight months and an adult who lived to be eighty might both appear to be in their thirties for all of eternity.

Even though the Bible does not tell us the answer to this question, there are several things that we do know for sure. The first of which is that our children will not exist in heaven as angels. Our pop culture has led many people astray with their false teaching that after a person dies they spend eternity on a cloud playing the harp. The Bible is clear that all the angels have already been created, and angels are not what humans become. Matthew 22:30 teaches that people in heaven will not get married, but rather, they will be like the angels. This passage does not say that we will become angels, but that we will have in common with angels the fact that we won't be given in marriage. Furthermore, Hebrews 12:22-23 explains that people in the New Jerusalem will be met by angels and the "spirits of righteous men made perfect." These verses make a distinction between angels and humans that have been made perfect in heaven and given a glorified body.

In heaven we will all have a glorified body (1 Corinthians 15:51-54; Romans 8:23; Philippians 3:21). Those who were blind on the earth will see, those who were mute will speak, those who were deaf will hear, and so on. Heaven will not be a place where senior citizens inch around with their walkers. Our bodies will be free from ailments and no longer be restricted by physical limitations.

In the verses listed in parenthesis in the previous paragraph, Paul wrote to the Christians in Rome and told them that their bodies would be redeemed at the resurrection. This means that our bodies will be set free from sickness, weariness, deterioration, and everything else brought on by the curse. He continued that thought in his letter to the Philippian Christians, telling them that their bodies would change from being vile to being glorious.

Because of this, I believe that my miscarried children will appear just as they were on the ultrasound yet be fully functioning beings in heaven. They will be able to walk and talk, run and play, and go about doing all of the other activities that a person would do in heaven. I believe that one day I will be able to pick them up and hold them, and even though I will miss out on that here on earth, I will be able to be with them eternally in heaven and not be limited by human finite limitations.

More importantly, today I believe they are worshipping at the feet of Jesus. When I get to heaven, I will worship the Lord, in part because I understand the depth of mercy and forgiveness that He has bestowed upon me. These children will never appreciate what it means to be forgiven for sins, but they will worship God for rescuing them from the heartache, sickness, and pain that comes from life on this earth. If there is one fact that should encourage during these difficult times, let it be the fact that our children will not have to go through difficult times.

Heaven's Nursery

The title for this book just came to me one day long before I had even considered writing it. I was trying to express some of the feelings that I was going through in a journal, and I wrote that I had "another child asleep in heaven's nursery." That phrase has stayed with me in the back of my mind ever since.

With that said, I want to be very clear: the Bible never mentions heaven having a nursery. This is something that the pastors at our church refer to as being part of our "biblical imagination." I stress this point because I never want to be found guilty of teaching something that is not found in the Word of God.

Yet in my biblical imagination, I have often pictured all of these children sleeping in a nursery like the ones at a hospital's labor and delivery unit. I can't help but smile when I think about my Father God looking after my little ones until their mother and I can go up there to be with them.

This imagery came more to life for me after the birth of our daughter, Reagan. The events of the day, including the C-section, had taken a toll on my wife, and she was in a considerable amount of pain in the post-operation room. Reagan had been taken to the well-baby nursery, but I stayed with Alicia in post-op until she was ready to be moved to her recovery room. In the meantime, Reagan was being taken care of by a nurse until we got to the new room.

Alicia was not physically able to take care of a baby that was only a few hours old, so Reagan spent her first night in the nursery; in the morning when we were ready, we got to get our little girl. That is the scene I have played over and over in my mind: our children asleep in heaven's nursery, being taken care of by God until the time comes for us to go be with them.

Your children are there too.

Don't worry. They are in good hands. In fact, they are in God's hands, asleep in heaven's nursery.

What about My Aborted Baby?

So you have come to this point in the book and followed the case for the existence of a Creator God, his heaven, the life you conceived, and the age of accountability. A logical question that might follow would be, "What about my aborted baby? Did he go to heaven?"

If that is the question of your heart, then let me assure you that, yes, your child is in heaven. Hopefully by this point you realize that it was a mistake to have an abortion, and while there may be consequences you face for the choice you made, those consequences will in no way be laid to the charge of your innocent baby.

A lost child is a lost child, no matter what events led to the loss. Just as we discussed in the previous chapter, all children who never lived to see an age of accountability will be found innocent before Jesus Christ and allowed into heaven.

In chapter three, the conclusion was made that life begins at the moment of conception; therefore, it is a personal conviction of mine that it is wrong to make a decision to end that life. If you share that same conviction now, there are a few things you need to understand. First, you may have chosen abortion before you realized why it is wrong. Don't worry; God is faithful to forgive all who confess their sin and turn from it (1 John 1:9).

But you may have chosen to have an abortion despite the fact that you knew it was wrong, whether to cover up a mistake or for fear of the future. Don't worry; God will be faithful to forgive you as well if you confess your sin and turn from it.

In a famous biblical account, there was a woman caught in the very act of adultery and brought before Jesus. When the crowd expected Jesus to give the order to have the woman put to death, Jesus surprised them all. When the law stated that this woman could be stoned to death (which was a form of capital punishment at the time), Jesus announced that whoever was sinless should throw the first stone at this woman. One by one these religious leaders dropped their stones and walked away.

Then Jesus gave the most incredible charge to this woman. He said that he did not condemn her, and he told her to go her way and not to commit the same sin again (John 8:11).

It is important to point out that Jesus is not soft on sin; in fact, he hates it. I am sure that there was still some form of punishment that came this woman's way, just not in the form that the crowd expected. The religious leaders in the story had actually broken the law themselves by bringing only the woman to Jesus. The law stated that both parties were to be punished equally, yet these men let the man off the hook (he may well have been in the crowd holding a stone). Jesus was not going to let this woman pay the price for a trap that was intended to put Jesus in a predicament.

But what is more important in this story is the fact that Jesus did not let the woman off the hook and send her on her merry way back to her life of fornication. Instead, Jesus told her to leave her life of sin behind. She had been given another chance.

That is where you now find yourself. If you acknowledge that you have made a mistake, simply ask the Lord to forgive you. If you have done your part, he will do his part. You are forgiven; now go and sin no more.

God is the God of second chances, of new beginnings. Just ask Jonah, Jacob, Peter, Paul, and almost everyone else in the Bible. You are not to wear a scarlet letter for the rest of your life. In God's eyes, no sin is worse than any other, so one poor decision in your life is no worse than one bad thought, one sentence spoken as gossip, one lost temper, etc. God hates all sin equally but forgives all sin eternally.

If you have given your life to Christ and become a child of God, then one day you will be united with your child in heaven. One day you will know the answer to the questions you have been asking yourself, such as what your child looks like. More importantly, you will be able to spend eternity with your child in a place where the word *abortion* will never again be brought up.

And remember, in a world where many teach that abortion is the unpardonable sin, the only unpardonable sin is to reject Jesus Christ with your life. An abortion cannot send a person to hell; in fact, no one or no thing can send a person to hell. But if you are living your life for yourself and not for God, then you are choosing hell for yourself. If you have not yet done so, turn from your sin and make a decision to follow Christ with your life.

If You Are Considering Abortion

Maybe there is a woman or couple reading this that is considering abortion. Despite the fact that abortions have become so common in this country, it is difficult to get accurate information about the practice. There are too many young women that choose abortion without really knowing what they are getting into. In fact, many women have said that if they knew what was going to take place before their abortion, they never would have gone through with it. Because of that, I decided to include this chapter.

First, I believe it is beneficial to point out that there is an alternative to abortion. Even if you are not in the position to be able to raise this child (perhaps you are too young, too ill, or not financially able, and you have no support group to help you), you still do not have to abort him. You can give your child up for adoption and give him the chance to live his life.

There are critics of adoption that claim that these children are not given a chance in life, as many of them spend their entire childhood in orphanages. While that may be true, they are still alive and capable of rising above their circumstances and making something out of themselves (that is not a luxury that *aborted* children enjoy). Plus, it is not fair to ignore the number of children that are adopted into good families. Many of these children are allowed to have visits from their biological parents, and furthermore, they are privileged enough to be given a better shot at life.

People Who Were Adopted

For the people who think that a child put up for adoption might not get to enjoy life, consider these people who were adopted:

- Mark Shultz—Christian singer/songwriter whose music inspires millions
- Babe Ruth—professional baseball player who learned the sport at an orphanage from fellow orphans
- Dave Thomas—Wendy's founder and founder of Dave Thomas Foundation, an organization that helps make adoption cheaper
- George Washington Carver—born as a slave, became a chemist, invented peanut butter
- Alexander Hamilton—influential in America's independence; first Secretary of the Treasury and organizer of nation's financial system
- Steve Jobs—cofounder of Apple and inventor of the iPod

This list could go on with hundreds of names of people who made names for themselves. This list would also include NFL stars like Daunte Culepper, musicians like Faith Hill and Tim McGraw, Unites States President

Gerald Ford, actors like Melissa Gilbert and Marilyn Monroe, writers like Edgar Allan Poe, United States senators like Robert Byrd, and other politicians like South African President Nelson Mandela.

The point is this: don't rule out adoption because you think that your child might not have a good life. If you choose abortion, your child will never *have* a life.

Advocates of abortion like to use that as their battle cry: "Think of what a bad life your baby will have in an orphanage!" But you never hear them putting the shoe on the other foot. Consider some of the greatest problems in our country, like AIDS, cancer, and the decline of Social Security. The real question should be, "What if that baby you are thinking about aborting would grow up and find a cure for cancer or AIDS?"

What if a baby aborted back in the seventies was meant to be the one to cure cancer? We would have that cure *today*.

And then there is the Social Security problem. I heard a prominent senator say that in order to fix Social Security, we would need about 30 million more people paying into the system. Ironically, and quite sadly, it has been estimated that there have been fifty *million* babies aborted in this country since *Roe v. Wade* was passed.

The Process

The process of abortion will not be described in this book due to the graphic nature of the content, and most people reading this book won't want to read about the details. However, I believe that it is vitally important that anyone considering abortion first do research and find out exactly what is involved. If you are considering abortion, then you should first go to Google.com and type in "vacuum aspiration abortion procedure."

Is Abortion Okay to Save the Mother's Life?

Most people that are pro-abortion pretend that they actually hate abortion. They will use one of two lines of reasoning to perpetually justify their stance. The first line of reasoning is, "We *have to* keep abortion legal if it will save the mother's life," and the second is, "We *have to* keep abortion legal for the cases or rape and incest." Most (if not all) politicians on the left will claim that these are the reasons they want to keep abortion legal, and yet, oddly enough, they have never worked to pass any legislation that would only keep abortion legal for these two reasons.

It is hard to argue with the idea of performing an abortion to save the mother's life, but in reality, that does not need to be done. If there is a tragic situation in which only one of the two can survive, you should do whatever it takes to save the life that can be saved. For example, if the mother requires an emergency procedure before she is far enough along to deliver, then go forward with the procedure; if the child does not survive the procedure, this was not an abortion but an attempt to save one life instead of losing both.

One must keep in mind that as long as the mother has reached twenty-four weeks, then the child can be delivered. This obviously is not ideal, but it certainly should rule out abortion.

If the mother has not reached the twenty-four-week point yet, then the idea is always to save the life that can be saved. A doctor will assess the facts, like an ectopic pregnancy, which is harmful to the mother, but the child is already lost anyway. Or there might be cancer, in which case the mother's treatment would be too much for the baby to handle. In these cases, being pro-life means saving the mother's life. This is not abortion. Toxemia may cause the mother to go on bed rest, but this is not life threatening to the mother, and abortion should not be considered.

It should be noted that Dr. C. Everett Koop, former U.S. Surgeon General, said that in his thirty-six years as a pediatric surgeon he was never aware of a single situation in which an abortion was necessary to save the mother's life.

Is Abortion Okay in the Case of Rape or Incest?

The second line of defense most often used to justify abortion is if the mother is a victim of rape or incest. Granted, a rape victim did not plan on conceiving a child and having her life change in this way, but why have a second tragedy to try to cover up the first? Aborting the child does not undue the crime committed against her. Quite the opposite can be true: the baby can serve as a blessing that came from a tragedy.

Just like when dealing with adoption, children conceived via rape can still live a very happy, healthy life, rise above their humble beginnings, and contribute something great to society. A woman who conceives after a crime has no way of knowing if she is carrying the next Ronald Regan, Billy Graham, or Margaret Thatcher.

But that is only *if* there is a conception. Consider these facts presented in Randy Alcorn's concise defense of his views *Why Pro Life?* His research found that two consenting adults only have a 3-percent chance of conception from an act of intercourse, and this number is smaller when one party does not consent. Furthermore, less than 1 percent of abortions performed annually in this country stem from rape. Many women are able to prevent a pregnancy from taking place after they have been raped, which is not abortion. They are preventing pregnancy, not terminating.

In the case of incest, which usually entails a young girl being sexually abused by a relative, abortion still should not be considered. Why should a child have to die because his father made poor choices? No sane person would suggest killing the child of a bank robber, so why would we kill the pre-born child of a sex offender?

Just like there is a myth that many women have to have abortions because of rape, there is also a myth that children born of incest will have physical deformities. Both cases occur far fewer than most people think. But even if a child were going to have physical deformities, he is just as much entitled to life as any other person. If you don't believe me, get to know a person with physical deformities.

So if you are considering abortion, please reconsider.

Adoption is a great option.

For a testimony from a woman who chose abortion, please read the Testimonies.

Coping with Comments

This chapter will perhaps serve as a how-to manual for coping with the comments that you will no doubt hear during this time. Unfortunately, just like with any tragedy, many well-meaning people are going to feel as if they simply *have to* say something that will suddenly wash all of the pain away, especially the Christian friends and relatives who believe that they are supposed to have all of the answers.

If you are one of those friends or relatives, let me just tell you now there is nothing, absolutely *nothing*, that you can say that will assist in easing the suffering that your loved one is experiencing, so take the burden off of yourself. They just need you to be there for them right now, not to say something profound.

The morning after the worst night of my life was very difficult. We had only lived in Orlando a few short days and had just lost our first child. My wife and I had spent most of the night in the emergency room, and I had gotten almost no sleep. I had already agreed that I would help a friend with something before I went to work the next day, so I honored that commitment.

When I got there, he felt as if he had to say something, and the best he could come up with was, "So you're not gonna be a dad yet, huh?"

In my anger, I wanted to let him know exactly what I thought of his pitiful attempt at condolence, and maybe I would have if my broken heart had not overwhelmed me. In that moment, it took all of my restraint not to break down and cry.

What are we supposed to do in moments like that? Certainly we would be justified for any harsh comments we made in retaliation, right? Even a punch right in the nose seems mild, at best. However natural these responses may seem, they will not benefit us anything.

The comments you hear will hopefully not be as blunt as the one I heard from my friend, but you will most likely encounter some of these more common, pithy comments:

> Well, I guess it just wasn't meant to be.
>
> These things happen.
>
> At least you weren't too far along yet…
>
> Everything happens for a reason.
>
> Better luck next time!

By far the most insulting was the person who actually said to me (in church!), "Well, we want a healthy baby, and it sounded like this baby wasn't going to be healthy, so it's probably for the best."

My response to that person was, "So you're telling me that if this child were born handicapped, then you don't think I would have loved him?" She said that was not what she meant, but comments like those reveal the true thoughts of people that have never been in these types of situations.

When you hear these comments, you will naturally want to go off on the messenger, but that will not make you feel any better. I believe that most people would excuse what we say and how we say it, but that does not mean that God excuses it. There is nothing wrong with letting someone know that their comments are not helpful, but it needs to be said in a gracious manner.

A good way to educate a person this way is by saying something like this: "I know you don't have all the answers, and that's okay. I don't need you to try to fix this situation. I just need a hug right now." Don't forget these people really are trying to help you, so let them know exactly how they can be of help.

It is easy to harbor feelings of anger or resentment or bitterness toward these people, but those emotions must be let go of as you embrace forgiveness. Even if they never realize how cutting their comments are, and even if they never ask for forgiveness, we still have a biblical obligation to forgive them anyway (Ephesians 4:32).

Some of these people will go on to realize just how painful the loss of an unborn child can be. I have witnessed several people whose comments were less than comforting go on to lose a child themselves, and because the Lord had given me the power to forgive them, I was able to minister to them.

The greatest way that Christians can minister to people who have experienced loss is just to simply show them love. We don't need to try to sound philosophical or appear extra spiritual; we just need to be there, to listen, to hold their hand or give a hug, and pray for them.

The best example I have seen of someone doing this was Barry and Myra Bunn in Orlando. After our second miscarriage, they loved us like Jesus. It was therapeutic for my wife to just get out of our house, and they asked if we wanted to spend the night at their house. We accepted their offer and slept on their couches.

There was never a minute where they tried to explain to us why this had happened or offer any advice. They just gave a place to get away and, in essence, hide out from the comments that would soon come from other people.

There are some comments that are helpful during these times. We liked to hear from people who said, "I went through the exact same thing. I know what you're going through. Let me know if I can do anything for you."

I recently talked to a young lady who had just had her third miscarriage. I was able to tell her that we had three ourselves before the Lord blessed us with a beautiful, healthy little girl. She found comfort in that comment.

In the future, you may be in a situation where you can offer real help to someone who is experiencing exactly what you are experiencing right now. If so, love them like Jesus. Let them know that you will be there if they need anything, and more importantly, pray for and with them. Romans 5:3-5 reminds us that the trials that we go through can be used to bring about some good. Our trials can produce perseverance in our lives, and that perseverance leads to proven character and hope. We can use this as a means of encouragement when we see others begin to experience the same trials that we have been through.

My Advice

I can't close this book without including some advice from my own personal experiences. I am not attempting to heal any wounds with what I am about to say, but rather I strongly believe that what is written in this section is the reason that God led me to write this book to begin with.

You may not want to move forward with this final chapter until after you feel as if you have gotten stronger emotionally. You may just want to wait and then come back to this in a few weeks or months, but please, whatever you do, read this final chapter. It could make all the difference for you and future generations.

Statistically, most women will have at least one miscarriage in her life. I have heard many people in the medical profession suggest that the majority of women who think they have never experienced a miscarriage actually have and they just don't realize it. With home pregnancy tests being so readily available in the grocery stores and gas stations today, women are finding out much earlier that they are pregnant.

Imagine this scenario: a hundred years ago a woman suspects that she might be pregnant because she is three weeks late for her period. Without a home pregnancy test or ultrasound, she just waits it out. A week later she begins to bleed due to a miscarriage, but in her ignorance, she comes to the conclusion that she was just late and is now having her period.

The truth of the matter is that women's bodies don't know how to respond to her first conception. In many cases, her body's natural defense system will fight it off for fear that there is some type of infection. For other women, their bodies simply can't handle it. For a healthy pregnancy, there are thousands of things that must happen precisely right, and for most first-time conceptions, that just doesn't happen.

What usually does happen, however, is a successful second attempt. For most couples, the sixth week after a miscarriage (or after a D&C is performed) is the target week for a healthy conception. More often than not, women will have a miscarriage and then deliver a baby in less than a year.

Here is my point: don't give up. If you are parents who have lost a child to miscarriage, as soon as you feel that you are ready, try again. You may not want to try again right away, and that is perfectly fine. Take time to heal both physically and emotionally, but don't give up.

Husbands, your wives might say something along the lines of, "I'm never going to get pregnant again." Don't get sad or upset with her. She is going through a lot, and remember, her hormones are still going crazy. Your role is to help her get through this time and then encourage her to try again when she is ready.

Wives, your husbands may not show any emotion, or they might say something downright stupid in an attempt to make you feel better. Don't get frustrated with them. A man wants to help his hurting bride, and it bothers him if there is something beyond his control. Also, men struggle with showing emotion—a lack of tears does not indicate a lack of hurt. You might never see him cry.

If you have had more than one miscarriage, I know how hard it is to keep hoping that each time will be "the one." In our culture, we have put so much emphasis on a husband and wife creating life, but in reality, they are only the agents that God uses to bring forth the life that he creates. The point is, as long as you are able to try, then keep trying. Keep hoping. Keep praying. Keep believing.

You never know which time might be successful, but you are guaranteed a zero-percent success rate if you stop trying altogether. Don't give up. The questions of "Why?" do not have to be answered right now (or ever). As Christians, we must accept the sovereignty of God, which means that God is absolutely in control of every situation and nothing happens that God did not either plan or allow.

One of the hardest questions to try to answer is why God would allow something tragic to happen. In some situations, after a period of time has passed, we may be fortunate enough to see the answer. It is that "aha" moment when suddenly it all makes sense and we see how we actually benefitted from a tragedy.

Sometimes God just doesn't make sense to us, and no matter how much we can try to study him and understand his ways, we will never fully comprehend it all. In fact, in Isaiah 55:8-9, God tells us that his thoughts and his ways are so much higher than ours, so just when we think that we have God figured out, he blows us away.

And the things that seem incomprehensible to us in our finite minds are really just one puzzle piece in the greater scheme of our lives. Some pieces of the puzzle don't look good to us, but God promises that he works it all out in our favor if we really love him (Romans 8:28).

Another verse that Christians love to quote to each other for encouragement is Jeremiah 29:11, which says, "For I know the thoughts that I think toward you, saith the Lord, thoughts of peace, and not of evil, to give you an expected end." This verse is saying that God has good plans in store for his people.

But so many Christians who never go through hard times cannot fully appreciate the promise of that verse. That was not some "health, wealth, and prosperity" preacher delivering those words during times of abundance. Actually, Israel had been taken captive and had all but been destroyed. This was a prophecy that *after a long period of suffering* God would step in and carry out his good plans for his people.

No one is exempt from hard times. They will come. What is important to know is that when you experience these hardships, God is going through them with you. He hasn't forgotten about you, and he wasn't asleep when all this happened. You have to accept the fact that what you are going through is a part of his plan for your life.

Nobody understands the pain of losing a child like God does. And just like with you, the child that God lost was innocent. But it was through the death of Jesus that our sin problem was solved, so God allowed his only Son to die as a substitution for us and our children.

So you can cry out to God during this time of pain. He has been there, and he knows better than anyone what you need to get through this time. Better than that, he, more than anyone, is *able* to give you what you need during this time.

Testimonies

One of the things that has helped me personally during these hard times has been the testimonies of those who have gone through similar circumstances. Just knowing that I was not alone in what I was feeling was a great comfort. Beyond that, there were many Christians who were able to pray for me and encourage me. And when I was in my darkest hour, I was able to see that there was a light at the end of my tunnel.

But maybe you do not know of anyone who has gone through similar trials, or maybe it is just too difficult to have that conversation in person just yet. For those reasons, I have included the testimonies of people who have experienced the pain of miscarriage and stillbirth. There is also a testimony from a woman who chose to have an abortion and has regretted that decision ever since.

As they share their stories, I hope you will find some degree of comfort as you realize that you are not alone.

Testimony #1:
Stillbirth–Chuck and Carol, Georgia

It was the spring of 1995, and we lived in Birmingham, Alabama. We were expecting our second child, a girl we had named Rachel. One night about three weeks before Rachel's due date, we got a call from Chuck's mother telling us that Chuck's dad had been taken to the hospital. The doctors didn't know if he would make it through the night. We quickly packed and drove south to Montgomery, Alabama.

We were so thankful that Chuck's dad came home from the hospital after a ten-day stay. Chuck's dad had pulmonary fibrosis and a potassium imbalance, and he was unable to care for himself. We spent most of the last three weeks of Carol's pregnancy in Montgomery, helping out and commuting occasionally to Birmingham to spend some time in Chuck's office. We were able to find someone to help Chuck's mother while we were going to be in Birmingham for the delivery.

Carol's pregnancy had been a normal one and had been full of the hopes and dreams of anticipating a new baby. Carol had her last doctor's appointment two days before the due date. Carol took our four-year-old daughter, Kathleen, with her to the appointment. The doctor checked Carol and started to check the baby's heartbeat and could not find one. An ultrasound was quickly performed and confirmed that there was no heartbeat.

We met at the hospital and then decided to go home and call family members and make other arrangements. We also had to explain to Kathleen what had happened. We returned to the hospital later that evening. The next day, May 31, 1995, Rachel Lacey Dowd was stillborn.

One week after Rachel was born, we were back in Montgomery to help care for Chuck's dad. We spent the majority of June and July going back and forth between Montgomery and Birmingham. It helped in some ways that we had the distraction of being needed in Montgomery, but in some ways it delayed the grieving process. Chuck also had to make a trip to the emergency room during this time with an attack of kidney stones as we were preparing for Kathleen's birthday party.

After a time of improvement, Chuck's dad had a fall and returned to the hospital. He went to be with the Lord on August 6, 1995.

We experienced a pain so deep that summer that only God's goodness and love could carry us through. Even in all our sadness and pain, God's goodness was more evident than it had ever been before. God showed his love to us through his Word, our supportive church family, and our friends.

The entire first year was very difficult. We wanted Rachel to be remembered, and sometimes it was more difficult when no one spoke about her than it was to talk about what had happened. Carol always liked it when people would use Rachel's name in conversation and she could talk about it instead of avoiding the subject.

For several years after that, Mother's Day and baby dedications at church proved to be a painful reminder of our loss. We found that it was easier to just go out of town for Mother's Day. If there was a baby dedication at church, we would enter the service after the baby dedication had ended.

There are moments when we think of a current milestone that she would be achieving in her life, such as beginning school or applying for her driver's permit. These moments were very difficult at first, but time has helped soften the emotion to more of a bittersweet thought of what might have been. God has blessed us with friends that are willing to listen and to encourage us during these times.

Three things that we have gained through this experience are:

1. The ability to see God's hand in everything, even the smallest of things.
2. An understanding that God is in control even when it seems like he is not.
3. A stronger marriage.

We realized early on that we could make a choice in our lives to continue grieving, or we could accept the peace that God meant for us to have. A very helpful verse was John 16:33, which states, "These things I have spoken unto you, that in me ye might have peace. In the world ye shall have tribulation. But be of good cheer; I have overcome the world."

Carol has had the opportunity to share her experience in a worship service and also to share personally with other women who have faced a similar loss. She was able to share about how God has helped her to continue on. As the Bible says in 2 Corinthians 1:4, God comforts us in all our troubles so that "we may be able to comfort them that are in any trouble by the comfort wherewith we ourselves are comforted of God."

Since we lost Rachel in 1995, God has blessed us with two more wonderful children. We thank God for our family and what he is teaching us through all four of our children. Even though we don't understand why we lost Rachel, we are thankful for our faith in God and how it has been strengthened through this experience.

Testimony #2:
Miscarriage–Greg and Stacy, Alabama

Because I teach a youth Sunday school class, I often hear the word *love* being thrown around so loosely that it sometimes bothers me when I hear it. What does a teen know about true love? That is not to say a teen can't find true love, but knowing now that true love comes only from God and only after having the love of Christ in me do I truly know what love is all about. It took me several years of throwing this *love* word around before I finally experienced it for myself.

Only after going through several ups and downs in relationships, many heartaches, and coming to the point where I was emotionally numb did I finally find true love. The one obstacle that got me to this point in my life was right after my wife and I experienced a miscarriage with our first child. The main problem was that we weren't married yet. This, among many other problems at that point in our lives, was the hardest thing I have ever had to deal with.

It started out with us meeting at church—the one place you would think would be a great starting point. Well, it would have been, but I was just going to church to pick up pretty girls. It may have been wrong, but that is how it happened, and I did find the best-looking girl of them all. We had started quickly getting to know each other, with neither of us taking life too seriously. I knew from the first date that she would be the one I wanted to spend my life with, but I still didn't love her with the love of Christ. If I had loved her that much, then I would have never had sex before marriage. I would have displayed respect and showed real maturity, but I did not. We started off fairly quickly since we thought we were in love, sneaking around, fooling around, and never thought about the consequences of our actions.

We would party at my house with friends or go out to bars, where we would get so drunk we could not even stand up. We thought our love was strong enough that if we were to get pregnant that would be okay. We started experimenting even more, almost trying to get pregnant, and that is just what happened. We weren't ready for what was about to happen in our lives, but God had a plan. We found out we were pregnant and kind of freaked out, but we knew we were in love, and nothing could stop us. The next step was extremely tough, and that was telling our parents the big news. We told her parents first, and it was gut wrenching and almost impossible to describe. Her mom and dad were both strong and quiet and did not say much, but it was the loudest silence I had ever heard. In fact, the tears in her dad's eyes said it all. I will never forget that. I hope and pray I never have to go through that with my children.

Sure her parents liked me as a person, but look what I had done to their daughter. They wanted us to quickly get married so that it would not look so bad in the public eye, and even though we knew we were going to get married at a certain point, that wasn't the time. So next we told my parents, who were surprisingly very accepting, but still I can never describe the disappointment in their eyes. Since they were "super Christians," they tried their best to encourage us and give us some good advice. I knew, though, that they did not approve of my actions, but if God can forgive all sins, then they could forgive ours.

We took it in from all sides and went with the flow. I went on living like I already had been—drinking every night, still going out partying at times, and every so often I might go to church. What happened next was even tougher and by far the hardest thing I have ever had to deal with in my entire life. She woke me up early one morning hurting and bleeding and said we needed to go to the hospital. We found out there that we had lost the baby. Even now thinking about it brings tears to my eyes.

We were torn apart, hurting like never before. We had already made plans for the arrival, planned out our lives with a new baby, but God knew better. It was tough, and I didn't know what to do; there was nothing I *could* do. She was in a state of depression and couldn't get her mind off the baby. I didn't turn to God right away, but fortunately for me, she did. The only problem was the rumors around town that may have started at the church. It was rumored that we had an abortion, which was completely false. It hurt my wife more that certain people from our church looked down on us because of the rumors, but we were not at church for people. We were there for God or an answer to our nightmare.

She dragged me to church for weeks. I think she thought if she could go to church enough that God might forgive her and bless her with another baby. She was ready to get started trying to have another one, and we did, still not married though. I was still drinking every night, but I had slowed down going out quite as much. We were slowly going to church more and actually started going to Sunday school, but we hadn't quite surrendered to God. We started making new friends with people who were truly saved and who had given their lives to Jesus Christ, and they were spreading their love onto us.

We were doing better but still holding onto a few things. For one thing, I was still drinking, but it had slowed, and we were still living together out of wedlock, so we decided it was time to tie the knot. We wanted our pastor to marry us, and to do that he required premarital counseling. We started our first session, and all went well, but something happened in the second session. He informed us that if he were to marry us, we couldn't be living together. So we did what we thought was right and that was to get married in the sight of God in our pastor's office, and later we would have a ceremony for our friends and family.

It was the best thing we could have ever done. Not too long later, after many prayers from others and prayers of my own, it hit me one day during the morning worship service that I needed God. I knew the sacrifice his Son, Jesus, had made for me, and I wanted to serve him with all that I had. And I did and still do. After making this decision, the most important decision any one person could ever make, we were happier than we had ever been in our relationship. We had the wedding ceremony two months after getting married in our pastor's office, and we went on our second honeymoon, the more expensive one.

The first time was just for one night in the mountains, just to celebrate our marriage the right way. We made love that night, married, the way God had intended it to be. And on our second honeymoon, we found out that we were pregnant again. The miracle in all this was that we traced back the time of conception, and God blessed us with our beautiful daughter the very night we set things right in God's eyes and got married. We had tried to get pregnant on our own, but we weren't living like he wanted us to, and we paid the price for our sins.

Only after all the pain and all the heartaches could God take something so tragic and turn it into something so perfect. That was God's love, that was God's plan, and it was perfect. A lot of times teenagers do not realize what true love is all about. I know I didn't, but it comes by putting God first before anything or anyone else. Then it all falls into place just like my life has. I now have two beautiful children, and I thank God for them every day. My relationship with my wife, my children, and basically everyone I know is better because of my relationship with God. God knew—God knows—if only we allow him to show us the way, through faith he will direct our path.

Tommy Mann

Testimony #3:
Abortion–Margaret Scirrino, New York

The following testimony is from Margaret Scirrino from an organization called Priests for Life, which is a pro-life group out of Staten Island, New York, that works to educate people on what abortion really is like. Margaret shares a lot of the private details in her life, which helps people relate to her suffering. But her story is not all sad; listen as she shares how God brought healing into her life through his forgiveness. Here is her story:

I was brought up Catholic, but I strayed away from God in my adolescent years, becoming sexually active at the young age of sixteen, and when I was seventeen, I became pregnant. The boyfriend I had been with for a couple of years was older than me, and in my mind, I thought we would marry. But his response was "Get rid of it. It's no big deal; get an abortion."

Although I had never heard anything about abortion, I just knew it was a terrible thing, but I was petrified to go to my father and thought he would throw me out, and I couldn't hurt my mom this way.

So being afraid to run away and do this all by myself, I had an abortion. A friend took me to the gynecologist; I can still see his face. He told me there was nothing to cry about; it was only a blob of cells. I remember that day that I went for the abortion. I cried all the way to the mill, was dropped off in front, and the boyfriend waited in the car outside. I sat inside the waiting room with tears streaming down my face—not one person offered me a choice or told me where I could get any help. When they prepped me and put me on that cold table with the lights glaring down on me, I felt like it was me that was going to die. And when I woke up, I was so sick. I was bleeding terribly. In pain, I felt so empty, guilty, ashamed, and afraid.

The abortion didn't relieve anything; in fact, it made me worse. There was no going back; this couldn't be undone. To this day I feel panic when I go to the gynecologist or get an IV.

The baby I aborted was tiny, seven ounces and two and a half inches tall, with little feet, a little face, organs that worked, and who could suck its thumb, cry silently, and whose brain was fully formed. She felt the pain of being brutally ripped apart and betrayal and the hurt from the one she should have been most safe with.

When I got home, I had to make-believe there was nothing wrong. Instead of going to school for the next week, I went to a friend's house, lay down on her bed, and cried every day. I finally got it together, and life went on. I stopped going to church. I was afraid to go to confession, and I was feeling that I didn't belong. I went from being a very bright and energetic student to just getting through high school and not going on to college; my drive for life was gone.

After a few years, I went on to marry a different man, out of a desperate search for a normal life. Unfortunately, it quickly became abusive. But I became pregnant by my first anniversary. Throughout my pregnancy, I was so afraid that I would lose the baby because of that abortion, and I had bleeding problems. When I felt the life growing inside me, in my mind was how I had killed my poor first baby.

During that second pregnancy I had hemorrhaging problems and felt it was because of the abortion—that God was going to take this baby from me as I had taken one from him.

My healing began during the time I cared for my mom as she suffered with terminal cancer. I started reading Scripture and really praying hard. My husband resented my helping my mother and became even more abusive. I finally got a restraining order against him. His anger was so fierce, and after I won a custody battle in the courts, he managed to alienate my three children against me.

I finally had to let them go and live with their father, as I was left with no control of them. For a few years, they wanted nothing to do with me because of his prompting. Deep inside I felt that God was allowing this because I had had the abortion. I had destroyed one of his children, and now he was taking the ones I knew and loved away from me. I was becoming sick from the guilt and the anger—stomach pains, migraine headaches, even skin problems.

I had started turning more to God, and I was brought down to my knees. I started really seeking God, and one morning while reading Scripture—Song of Songs—I experienced this overwhelming feeling of love, like it came down from heaven. It was an intense heat sensation that lingered and slowly traveled my entire body, from my head down to my toes, inside and out. I know it was Jesus showing me that he loved me and he was with me.

I started going to church and prayer groups. God led me to my final healing; he showed me that he had forgiven me, and now I understood that he really could forgive me of the horrible sin of abortion.

I went on to a healing from abortion seminar, shared with other women, named my baby "Hope," and gave her the spiritual burial in place of what actually happened. You see, my baby had been thrown in the garbage; after the fact, I learned that is what they do.

Ironically, my daughter called me and was in the same predicament that I was in at the same age of seventeen. She wanted to come back to live with me. She was pregnant, and her father was trying to force her to have an abortion. She came back to live with me, and with trust in God, I fought for the baby's life, and we gave birth to Megan, now seven. Megan is truly a gift. I can't imagine life without her here.

Testimony #4:
Loss of a Ninety-Nine-Day-Old Baby— Jared and Lacy, South Carolina

My wife, Lacy, and I got married on June 21, 2008. We had talked about it and figured we would spend about a year to ourselves, and then hopefully we would be able to get pregnant. God apparently had other plans for us, and in early September 2008, we found out we were expecting. We had a few problems early on, and that had us a little uneasy. My family hasn't had the best luck with babies. My mom lost a baby to miscarriage before I was born and another to still birth when I was a child. My first cousin and his wife lost twins because they were born at twenty-three weeks and were not to a point of viability. Then November 2007 rolled around, and my stepbrother and his wife had a baby boy at twenty-four weeks and a day. He lived for two weeks and passed away in the NICU due to an intestinal issue that caused an infection. As if that wasn't enough, in May of 2008, my brother and his wife were seven months into their pregnancy and one night realized that the baby wasn't kicking. They went to the hospital and got the dreaded news that there was no heartbeat. Of all days for that to happen, it was Mother's Day.

So of course every little issue that we had was going to scare us to death. But we also looked at it like, "what are the chances of this happening again?" We made it through the first trimester with some sickness and a little blood but no major issues. I told Lacy that if we could just make it to twenty-four weeks that everything was going to be fine. We hit the twenty-four-week mark, and we were so excited.

On January 31, 2009 (twenty-four weeks, six days), Lacy went into labor in the middle of the night. We didn't realize that she was in labor, but we went on to the hospital just to be safe. We thought they would just give her some medicine and send her home and everything would be fine. After all, I had a softball tournament the next day, and she had a maternity fair at the hospital that she was going to. Yeah, all those plans were changed when Alayna Renee Taylor was born at 7:20 a.m. She weighed one pound, twelve ounces when she was born, and she was twelve inches long. There are a lot more details to this story, and if you would like to read all of them, day by day, you can visit www.caringbridge.org/visit/alaynataylor.

Alayna did great for the first six weeks. She was growing like a weed, she was taking her feeds well, she was off her oxygen, she was enjoying us holding her, and she was starting to transition into wearing clothes and soon was going to be moved out of the incubator. Then one morning we came in, and she had become very swollen. She was back on her oxygen, and no one seemed to know why. She continued to swell over the next several days, and various things began to happen to her over the course of the next couple months. Her heart rate went up, we found out she had a tear in her stomach, she had two separate stomach surgeries, her kidneys began to fail, she went on peritoneal dialysis, her liver began to fail, and finally she got a blood disorder that she was not able to overcome. Alayna passed away on May 9, 2009, the day before Mother's Day.

When something like this happens, it's so hard to see how anything good can come of it. Through it all, Lacy and I continued to give God the glory for everything that he was doing even if we didn't understand it. We had watched God perform five separate miracles on our little girl. A few days after her stomach surgery, she had swollen so much that the fluid inside her body was choking out her lungs and not allowing her to breathe. The doctors and respiratory therapists were scrambling around, trying to figure out what to do. Lacy and I stood there and watched as fluid began to leak out of the incision in her stomach. Fluid just continued to flow out of her stomach until she could breathe again. We couldn't see God physically doing anything, but we knew that his hand was at work with her little body that day. It was nothing the doctors did; it was just something that God did. Another night Alayna had just had some tubes put in her lungs to keep fluid out of her lungs, and everything seemed to be going well. Then all of a sudden her heart stopped beating. They tried to revive her for over thirty minutes. They finally told us that they could continue trying to revive her but she may have permanent brain damage. The other option was for them to stop, and we could hold her as she passed away. We decided that we wanted to hold her. As the nurse turned to hand her to us, Alayna's heart rate jumped up to 120 beats per minute (bpm). She had no heart beat for thirty minutes; then all of a sudden it was 120 beats per minute. That was the amazing hand of God! After all the dust settled that night, we had nurses and respiratory therapists one by one come by and tell us that they had never seen anything like what they had just witnessed. One nurse told us that in thirty years of nursing, she had never seen anything like that. Even the doctor came to us and told us that they had done everything they knew to do based on experience and the training they had received. But in the end, they realized that it was out of their hands. He couldn't be more right because it was in God's hands. The last miracle we saw was when the Lord took her home to heaven. Our baby girl was finally healed.

At Alayna's funeral, our pastor talked about the impact that Alayna's life had. Through the CaringBridge website, we had over one hundred thousand visitors in just over three months of her hospital stay. We had people tell us that because of the faith and love we had shown, they had rededicated their lives to Christ. We had people who said they had grown in their faith because of the witness we had shown. We even had people tell us that because of our faith in Jesus, they had come to know him. That is such an amazing thing. Our pastor said that Alayna lived for ninety-nine days, which at the time we didn't realize. During the service, he said he wondered if he had made the impact in his whole life that Alayna made in just ninety-nine days. I wonder myself if I have made the impact in my 10,222 days on this earth that my baby girl made in just 99 days. It's definitely something for each of us to think about. What kind of impact has your life had on others?

There isn't a day that goes by that I don't think about my "Alayna Bug," and there probably won't be a day for the rest of my life that I won't think about her. Do I ask myself all the time why it was her time to go home with the Lord? Yes, all the time. Unfortunately, I won't know that answer until I am in heaven myself. It could be that Alayna's time here on earth was completed. The job that God sent her here to do was done. Maybe the whole reason Alayna was here was so that someone could be saved through her story. I don't know. I have found, though, that the best way for me to cope is to understand that God doesn't make mistakes. God is perfect, and his plan is perfect. Lacy and I were blessed with amazing families and amazing friends who helped us through the difficult times. We had a lot of prayer warriors praying for us. Don't be afraid to ask people to pray for you. You can really feel the power of prayer when something like this happens. Most importantly, don't give up. Every situation is different, but we have found that if we focus more on him and doing his work, we are so much more blessed. Through this ordeal, we have been blessed with new friendships, a new job, and a new ministry. We have now started a Neonatal ICU ministry to help provide hope to families who are going through the same things we went through. Our motto throughout Alayna's time here was praise and pray. Praise God for everything that he did for her and every day we had with her. Pray for continued grace, mercy, and love to be poured out on sinners like us. So fittingly, we named our ministry Praise & Pray Ministries.

Visit us at www.praiseandpray.org. Our hope is to provide care packages to the families who are sitting in the same rocking chairs we sat in. At the same time, we want to show them that through prayer and faith you can pull through the most difficult times in your life, even if things don't turn out how you want them to. We're very excited about this ministry and hope that the Lord will truly bless it. Please pray for us. We will be out doing his work while Alayna is asleep in heaven's nursery.

Appendix

Maybe you have come to the end of this book and you find yourself wanting more information. Here are a few resources that may be helpful:

If you are pregnant

If you feel like you need someone to talk to please contact us at www.tommymannministries.com. You can also find help at www.adoption.com and www.crisispregnancy.com.

For healing

Here are some websites that offer networking, newsletters, blogs, and others ways to help heal:

www.mend.org
(Mothers Enduring Neonatal Death)

www.bigtent.com/groups/naomiscircle
(Always a Dad support group)

www.facesofloss.com

www.theamethystnetwork.com

http://www.facebook.com/OfficialHealingAfterInfantLoss

www.nationalshare.org

Tommy Mann

In loving memory

These websites offer ways to memorialize your baby:

www.nowilaymedowntosleep.com

www.angelbracelets.com

www.abutterflystouch.org

Books

Here are some other books that may be helpful:

Safe in the Arms of God, John MacArthur
www.gty.org

I'll Hold You in Heaven, Jack Hayford
www.jackhayford.org

Mommy, Please Don't Cry, Linda Deymaz
www.mommypleasedontcry.com

To donate

Maybe you want to make donations to organizations that are fighting for cures or ministering to those who are hurting. Here are some great groups to consider:

www.marchofdimes.com

www.uchospitals.edu/specialties/obgyn/pregnancy-loss/

www.sweetpeaproject.org

www.praiseandpray.org

www.halemultimedia.com/starlegacy/

listen|imagine|view|experience

AUDIO BOOK DOWNLOAD INCLUDED WITH THIS BOOK!

In your hands you hold a complete digital entertainment package. In addition to the paper version, you receive a free download of the audio version of this book. Simply use the code listed below when visiting our website. Once downloaded to your computer, you can listen to the book through your computer's speakers, burn it to an audio CD or save the file to your portable music device (such as Apple's popular iPod) and listen on the go!

How to get your free audio book digital download:

1. Visit www.tatepublishing.com and click on the e|LIVE logo on the home page.
2. Enter the following coupon code:
   08f3-ef61-3163-ab89-7dae-4d2f-acef-5ddb
3. Download the audio book from your e|LIVE digital locker and begin enjoying your new digital entertainment package today!